Discipleship

Training from the Master Disciple Maker

By J. Carl Laney

Dedication:

This book is dedicated to the memory of my mom and dad whose love and guidance helped make me into the person I am today, and to my grandchildren who make me very proud.

Proverbs 1:8-9

Copies available from CreateSpace.Com

Amazon.com and Amazon.co.uk

Copyright 2018 by J. Carl Laney

ISBN 1985790327

Printed in the United States of America

Table of Contents

Preface

Shortly after I began my teaching career at Western Seminary, I was asked to serve as interim pastor at a little Baptist church on the outskirts of Portland, Oregon. For my Sunday morning sermon series, I chose to preach from Jesus' Upper Room Discourse as recorded in John 13-17.

This classic text has become one of my favorite sections of God's Word to preach and teach over the last forty years. I have used John 13-17 as the text for sermons, Bible conferences, and articles. I have taught this text to students hiking with me in the Cascade mountains, to missionaries serving in Taiwan and to U.S. military men and women stationed in Europe. The Upper Room Discourse occupies a major section of my commentary on John's Gospel (Moody Publishers).

In this exposition of John 13-17 I have focused on Jesus' final discipleship instructions. Jesus spent three and a half years training eleven men whom He commanded to "make disciples of all nations" (Matt. 28:19). On the night before His death, Jesus gave them His final instructions that would enable them to carry out that mission. These instructions are just as applicable for disciples today as they were when they were first given. May you be challenged, encouraged and strengthened spiritually by the final discipleship instructions of Jesus, *the Master Disciple Maker.*

J. Carl Laney

Introduction: Biblical Discipleship

This book is devoted to a study of Jesus' final instructions to His disciples which He delivered in the Upper Room on the night before His crucifixion (John 13-17). In His final words, Jesus coached His disciples by explaining and applying essential principles for living on earth as His followers.

What does it mean to be a disciple? Reading the Gospels, we discover that Jesus wasn't interested in people simply becoming Christians. Believing certain things about Him was important, but not enough. The New Testament word "disciple" (*mathetes*) means "learner." Being a disciple in the biblical sense means being a follower of Jesus, learning from His words and His example. Discipleship was like an apprenticeship.

If someone wants to become an electrician, it is not enough to sit in classes and learn the principles of electricity. The prospective electrician must become an *apprentice* to a licensed and experienced electrician to learn the trade by listening, watching and doing. The distinguishing mark of an apprenticeship is that the teacher and the apprentice *spend time together.* It is in and through the *relationship* of the teacher and the apprentice that the knowledge and skills of the trade are transferred.

In the first century, young Jewish men who wanted to learn the Torah would seek out a "rabbi." This Hebrew term means "my master," and was a title of respect for a recognized Jewish teacher. But students wouldn't just go to a classroom and listen to the rabbi lecture. Rabbis taught by what they *did* as well as by what they *said*. The disciples of a rabbi paid special attention to a rabbi's actions as well as their words. And rabbis were particularly careful about their behavior, knowing that their behavior was considered as an example to follow—a pattern for life.

In the Jewish culture of the first century, there was no distinct boundary between a rabbi's deliberate pedagogical measures and "the teacher's way of life as a whole, for his behavior was taken as an example, as teaching."[1] As a case in point, when a rabbi commanded that a collapsed wall be replaced by a stretched cloth on the Sabbath, a second rabbi present as a guest, accepting that it was within his host's jurisdiction, turned away his head, lest his disciples gain the erroneous impression that he approved of this work being done on the Sabbath.[2]

The pattern of rabbis in the biblical period was to travel from village to village, teaching in synagogues, Jewish homes or even out of doors, in a village square or under a tree. Renown Jewish teachers were instructed by their oral tradition "to make many disciples" (Mishnah, *Avot* 1:1).[3] Following this tradition, Jesus chose twelve men to

---

[1] B. Gerhardsson, *Memory and Manuscript*, (Grand Rapids: Wm. B. Eerdmans, 1998), 185-87.
[2] Michael Griffiths, *The Example of Jesus*, (Downers Grove, Illinois: InterVarsity Press, 1985), 22.
[3] The Mishnah is the written record of the oral traditions of Judaism (200 B.C. – A.D. 200).

become His disciples. These men spent the next three and a half years with Jesus, traveling with Him, listening to His words, observing the pattern of His spiritual life, and being sent out on missions where they could practice what they were learning in their apprenticeship.

In the Gospels we often find Jesus taking time away from His public ministry to spend time with His disciples (Mark 3:7, John 3:22). By spending time with His disciples, Jesus was investing His life in theirs, providing opportunity for the twelve to ask questions, get answers, and learn ministry skills which would enable them to carry on His ministry after His death. The example of Jesus leads me to define discipleship as "companionship in preparation for leadership." Teaching can be done in a classroom. But *biblical* discipleship can only be done *in relationship*. During His three and a half years of earthly ministry, Jesus was in an apprentice relationship with twelve men, eleven of whom would be entrusted with disciplining the nations (Matt. 28:19-20).

On the evening before His death, Jesus met with His disciples in an upper room in Jerusalem for a Passover Seder. There He gave them some final discipleship instructions. Although they had spent more than three years with Jesus, the eleven disciples still had some questions. In His Upper Room discourse Jesus answers such questions as:

What is Christian service all about? Why is obedience to God's Word so important to Jesus? How does the Holy Spirit direct and encourage his followers? What can we depend on the Holy Spirit to do as believers declare the good news of salvation? What does it

7

mean to pray "in Jesus' name"? How can Jesus' followers cope with the hostility of an unbelieving world? What does it mean to "abide" in Jesus? Why did Jesus return to his Father in heaven after his resurrection? Will he return to the earth again someday? What is Jesus' greatest concern for his followers in the world today?

These questions are as relevant for 21st century disciples of Jesus as they were for the original eleven. In this book we are going to study Jesus' Upper Room Discourse in search for answers to these questions.

But before we begin the first chapter, I want to share with you an ancient principle of discipleship which is tucked away in a book written by the Hebrew scribe, Ezra. The words of Ezra have served as my philosophy for teaching the Bible for the last 40 years. Ezra 7:10 records, "For Ezra had set his heart to study the *Torah* of the Lord, and to practice it, and to teach His statutes and ordinances in Israel."

Ezra was a scribe of priestly descent who led a contingent of Jews back from Babylon to Jerusalem in 458 B.C. He was noted for being "skilled in the Law of Moses" (Ezra 7:6). But don't think that his ability to study and teach the Hebrew Bible came without effort. Ezra's knowledge and ability to teach were the result of persistent study and personal discipline.

In Ezra 7;10 the word translated "study" literally means "to seek." Ezra made the Law (*Torah*) of God his primary textbook—the source of his instruction. But Ezra was not just a theologian who pondered the attributes of God in some ivory tower. He determined in his heart to *practice* the truth he had learned. Ezra desired to be a "doer" of the Word (cf. James 1:22-25). He was committed to putting God's truth into practice. Ezra also determined to *teach* others the great truths he had learned and applied.

As disciples of Jesus, we are all teaches in some capacity, whether in some official position as a pastor or Bible study leader or as a parent, introducing Jesus to our children in the home. You may not be teaching in a formal classroom situation, but you communicate God's truth through your words and deeds to your children, friends, and other Jesus followers.

Don't miss the significance of the order set forth in Ezra 7:10—first "to study," then "to practice," and finally, "to teach." You cannot practice what you have not thoroughly learned, and you cannot teach what you have not personally applied.

My goal in writing this book is not merely to help you come to a greater understanding of the discipleship instructions which Jesus presented in the Upper Room (John 13-17), but also to encourage you to apply it, and ultimately, to teach others what you have learned. May the Lord be pleased to bless our efforts as we pursue this goal together—for his glory!

Chapter 1

Evidence for Prospective Disciples

John 20:20-31

How many times have you heard it said, "I'll believe it when I see it?"

Many doubting Thomases have declared these words with reference to Scotland's Lock Ness monster, or "Nessie" as she is affectionately referred to. Traditions concerning a monster in the *loch* (Scottish for "lake") go back to at least to the sixth century A.D. Over the years, thousands have reported seeing something in the loch, and some photographs have been taken. One classic photo shows what appears to be the long neck and small head of some mysterious creature.

Most scientists believe that there is no monster in Loch Ness and that reported sightings are the result of overactive imaginations influenced by the misidentification of waves or other common objects. Yet many people believe that the loch does contain some large, unknown aquatic creature. Scientific investigations have been conducted at Loch Ness to solve the mystery. Investigators have obtained films and sonar readings that suggest the possibility of there being some unknown aquatic creature in the loch. But the evidence is inconclusive and the controversy continues.

Do you believe in the Loch Ness monster? I must confess that I don't and won't until I see that monster swimming around in an aquarium! Like doubting Thomas, I will not believe until I see clear, irrefutable evidence— evidence that demands a verdict!

Our study of the Jesus' discipleship instructions from the Upper Room must begin with an investigation of some evidence presented to us by one who heard Jesus' discipleship instructions firsthand. Though the author of the fourth Gospel never identifies himself by name, personal references indicate beyond reasonable doubt that the writer is John the Apostle (cf. John 13:23; 21:20; 21:24).

Early church leaders, including Irenaeus, Theophilus of Antioch, Clement of Alexandria, Origen, and Tertullian, are in agreement with the biblical record, attributing the fourth Gospel to John the Apostle. In order to become of disciple of Jesus, learning from His words and example, we must first enter into a relationship with Him, believing what the Apostle John tells us about the Master Disciple Maker.

The Background of the Apostle John

In a court of law, it is important to establish the integrity of those called to the witness stand, so that the judge and jury may have confidence that what the witness affirms is true. Since personal testimony is only as credible as the one who presents it, we need to examine briefly the career of John the Apostle and his association with Jesus.

John was the son of Zebedee and brother of James. He was a partner with his father, his brother James, Andrew and Peter in a fishing business on the Sea of Galilee. His mother's name was Salome, as a comparison of the parallel passages of Matthew 27:56 and Mark 15:40 will show. His brother James was probably older since he is always named first. John was an early disciple of John the Baptizer, and followed Jesus after encountering Him at Bethany beyond the Jordan. He accompanied Jesus on His first tour of Galilee and later quit the fishing business, along with his brother James, to become a fishers of men.

James and John, along with Peter, were witnesses of Jesus transfiguration on the mountain. John occupied a place of privilege at the Last Supper as he was reclining at Jesus' right hand. He witnessed the trial and crucifixion of Jesus and assumed responsibility for His mother Mary after Jesus committed her to John's care. When he arrived at Jesus' empty tomb on Resurrection morning, John "saw and believed" (John 20:8).

After Pentecost, John became a leader in the early church. He was associated with Peter in a number of exciting events recorded in Acts (cf. Acts 3:1-11; 4:3-321; 8:14-25). John was regarded with Peter and James as a "pillar" in the early church at Jerusalem. Irenaeus writes that John later resided at Ephesus where he served as bishop and wrote his Gospel. Polycarp, bishop of Smyrna, had a personal acquaintance with John and relates a story which helps us appreciate his colorful character. According to the story recounted by Eusebius, John once entered the bathhouse at Ephesus and saw there the heretic Cerinthus who denied the deity of Jesus. John fled without bathing exclaiming, "Let us flee lest the bath should fall in, as long as Cerinthus, that enemy of the truth, is within!" (*Historia Ecclesiastica*, 4:14).

John wrote his Gospel while residing in Ephesus, probably around A.D. 85. From Ephesus he later wrote his first, second, and third epistles around A.D. 90. In the 15th year of the Emperor Domitian (A.D. 81-96), John became the victim of Christian persecution and was exiled to the island of Patmos, a small rocky island in the Aegean Sea off the coast of Asia Minor, about 35 miles southwest of Miletus. The island served as a place of banishment during the time of Roman rule. Victorinus, a third-century Christian martyr, records in his commentary on Revelation 10:11 that John wrote the Book of Revelation on Patmos (about A.D. 95/96), and was liberated when Domitian was assassinated in A.D. 96.

Upon his liberation from Patmos, John took up residence again in Ephesus and spent the remaining years of his life visiting the churches of southeast Asia (southeastern Turkey), ordaining elders and fulfilling his ministry. Irenaeus records that John lived in Ephesus until the time of the Emperor Trajan (A.D. 98-117). Polycrates, bishop of Ephesus (A.D. 189-198), writes that John was buried in Ephesus where stands the ruins of an ancient church dedicated to his honor.

All this information about John is perhaps more than you wanted to know. But it is important to know something about the witness to be able to believe what he says about Jesus. It is clear from his background that John can be regarded as a credible witness.

The Testimony of the Apostle John

In John 20:30-31, the Apostle John states the purpose of his Gospel and what he would like it to accomplish in the hearts and lives of prospective disciples. He writes, "Many other signs therefore Jesus also performed in the presence of the disciples, which are not written in this book; but these have been written that you may believe that Jesus is the Christ, the Son of God; and that believing you may have life in His name." Throughout his Gospel, John presents what he believes to be convincing evidence that Jesus is the Messiah of Israel and the Son of God.

The Evidence for Belief (20:30)

The evidence designed to bring readers to a verdict is set forth in verse 30. John refers to the "signs" performed by Jesus in the presence of the disciples. In Peter's sermon on the Day of Pentecost, he referred to Jesus as "a man attested to you by God with miracles and wonders and signs" (Acts 2:22). These attestations, or testimonies, which God performed through Jesus during His earthly ministry are referred to as biblical *miracles*.

The use of the word "miracle" stands in stark contrast to the secular use of the word which defines a miracle as any wonderful act or event. When Roger Staubach led the Dallas Cowboys to two touchdowns in less than two minutes to win the 1972 NFL Championship over the San Francisco '49ers, the feat was called a "miracle victory." The 1980 Holiday Bowl is famous for the furious fourth quarter rally and last second "miracle touchdown." With four minutes left in the game, the SMU Mustangs had a commanding 45-25 lead. But the game wasn't over and

BYU scored an amazing 21 points in the last 2:33 minutes of the game! The box office hit *Miracle* (2004) tells the inspiring and true story of Mel Brooks who led the U.S. Olympic hockey team to a victory over the seemingly invincible Russian team.

The biblical use of the word miracle is also in contrast with the popular religious use of the word which designates a miracle as any answer to prayer or divinely providential event. A popular television evangelist says, "Expect a miracle today!" A seminary student exclaims, "God worked a miracle! He provided money for my tuition next semester."

A Biblical miracle is, in essence, a supernatural work which transcends the ordinary laws of nature and is accomplished by God for a specific purpose—usually the authentication of God's revelation or representative. Four Greek words are used in the New Testament to refer to miracles. The Greek word *dunamis*, from which we get the words "dynamite" and "dynamic," can be translated "a mighty work of power." Biblical miracles are "God's dynamite"—dynamic demonstrations of His supernatural power. Another word used with reference to biblical miracles is *teras* translated "a wonder" or "a marvel." This word emphasizes the response of the people witnessing the event. Those who see a miracle are astonished and stand in wonder of it. The Greek word *ergon*, from which we get the word "erg" (a measure of work and energy), is the term used most often by Jesus when referring to His own miracles. From a divine perspective, they are merely His "works." Finally, the Greek word *semeion*, translated "sign" suggests that the miracles are not ends in themselves. They signify something.

Nicodemus was right on target when he said to Jesus, "Rabbi, we know that You have come from God as a teacher; for no one can do these signs that You do unless God is with Him" (John 3:2). The miracles of Jesus were leading Nicodemus beyond the works themselves to some great truth about the Miracle-worker! The miracles of Jesus are the "insignia" of His deity and messiahship. The word s*emeion* is the word used in John 20:30 and is the term most often employed by the apostle John to refer to Jesus' miracles.

What are the *signs* (or miracles) John refers to in 20:30-31? There are seven miracles recorded in John's Gospel, apart from the resurrection of Jesus and the miraculous catch of fish recorded in the epilogue of chapter 21. Each of these seven miracles reveals something significant about the person and work of Jesus.

1. The first of his miracles, changing pure water into wedding wine (2:1-11), demonstrates that Jesus has authority over the physical world. This miracle proves the statement in the prologue of John's Gospel identifying the Messiah Jesus as the Creator (1:3; cf. Col. 1:16).
2. The second miracle is the healing of the nobleman's son (John 4:46-54). This miracle demonstrates Jesus' authority over sickness and illustrates his healing ministry.
3. The restoration of the lame man at the pool of Bethesda (5:1-9) demonstrates Jesus' authority

over the Sabbath and presents him as a restorer of sin damaged humanity.

4. The feeding of the 5,000 is a very significant miracle in that it is the only one of Jesus' miracles recorded in all four Gospels (Matt. 14:13-23; Mark 6:33-46; Luke 9:10-17; John 6:1-14). This miracle demonstrates Jesus' authority over nature and proves that he has the power to provide for his own.

5. The miracle of walking on the water (6:15-21) showed that Jesus would be with his own and protect them in their time of need.

6. In John 8:12, Jesus claimed to be the Light of the Word. In the next chapter, he does a miracle to prove that claim—he gives sight to the man born blind.

7. Finally, the resurrection of Lazarus (chapter 11) proves his claim to have the power to give life and raise the dead (5:12, 27-28). By this miracle, Jesus is seen to be the giver of life.

Note that John was selective in the choice of the miracles he recorded in his Gospel. He writes, "Many other signs therefore Jesus also performed" (20:30). Of the thirty-six specifically recorded miracles found in the Gospels, John chose these seven as primary evidence for the truth that Jesus is the divine Messiah. And John does not stand alone in his testimony concerning the deity and messiahship of Jesus. These miracles were performed in the presence of His disciples (20:30). The miracles of John's Gospel can be attested by others. They serve as convincing evidence that Jesus is who He claimed to be—the Messiah of Israel and Son of God.

The Goal of Belief (20:31a)

The Apostle John has presented the miracles as exhibit "A" in the case concerning Jesus. They are not merely intended to "liven up" the story. They are purposeful. We read, "But these have been written that you may believe" (2-0:31). The miracles recorded by John are designed to elicit belief in the *hearts* and minds of prospective disciples.

John's Gospel has been called "the Gospel of belief." The word "believe" (*pisteuo*) is used approximately ninety-eight times in the book and essentially means to "trust." It never means mere assent to a proposition but involves a personal response and commitment. A story about a chicken and a pig illustrates this concept. They left the farm to seek their fortunes. When they came to a country restaurant, the chicken conceived a great plan. The chicken said to the pig, "Why don't we go to work for the restaurant? We can provide the breakfast ham and eggs!" The pig thought for a time before replying. "No," he responded. "For you that would involve a mere contribution, but for me it would mean total commitment!" Biblical belief is *trust*. It is total commitment.

Ann Seward of Portland, Oregon, had an opportunity to exercise the biblical concept of belief (*trust*) when she was asked to co-star with high-wire artist Philippe Petit at the opening of the Portland Center for the Performing Arts. Her stage was an 80 ft. wire strung between the new theaters building and the Arlene Schnitzer Concert Hall. Placing her life in the hands of Philippe Petit, she clung to his back as Petit walked the wire high above the streets of Portland. She commented later, "I think that one of the most beautiful things about the performance was that it took a lot of trust—absolute trust. Here it is—I'm putting my life in someone else's hands and trusting the crowd not to do anything to distract him." This kind of *trust* is what John has in mind when he uses the word "believe."

There are several words which John uses in his Gospel as synonyms for "belief." In John 1:12, he speaks of "receiving" Christ. "But as many as received Him, to them He gave the right to become children of God, even to those who believe in His name." The word "receive" suggests a welcoming of Jesus in contrast to those who would reject Him and what He stands for. In John 3:36, "believing" is linked in a parallel relationship with "obeying." "He who believes in the Son has eternal life; but he who does not obey the Son shall not see life, but the wrath of God abides on him." Those who truly believe the Son will obey the Son. This suggests that belief is more than passive opinion. It involves personal response and commitment to an authority—Jesus, the Son of God.

Finally, in John 15:1-11, "believing" in Jesus is described as "abiding" in Him. John says in his first epistle, "Whoever confesses that Jesus is the Son of God, God abides in him, and he in God" (1 John 4:15). As we will see in our study of John 15:1-11, in John's writings "abiding in Christ" is virtually equivalent to "believing in Jesus."

The next time you share your faith with a prospective disciple, explain what it means "to believe." True *belief* in Jesus is trusting Jesus, welcoming Him into your life, committing yourself to an abiding relationship with him marked by obedience.

The Content of Belief (20:31b)

The real key to "belief" is its *content*. Some people think that it doesn't really matter what religious convictions they hold—just so they are sincere. Sincerity, however, is not enough. Perhaps you remember the "Peanuts" cartoon in which Charlie Brown was returning from a disastrous baseball game. He had a dark cloud over his head and a dejected expression on his face. The caption read, "184 to 0! How could we lose when we were so sincere?" Well, Charlie Brown, sincerity is not enough in baseball, and it is not enough to win the game of life. What you believe—not belief alone—is crucial to saving faith!

John tell us in 20:31 that the miracles recorded in his Gospel are designed to lead the readers to believe that Jesus of Nazareth is the "Christ, the Son of God." Let's consider these two significant terms which are used throughout the New Testament to refer to Jesus. The first term, "Christ" (*Christos*), may be literally translated "anointed one" and corresponds to the Old Testament term "Messiah." This Hebrew word is used in the Hebrew Bible and in later Judaism with reference to the central figure of Jewish expectation (Dan. 9:25-26). According to Scripture, the Messiah, a member of the tribe of Judah and descendant of David (Gen. 49:10; Ps. 110:1), is the heir to the promises given to David in 2 Samuel 7:12-16. He will receive the throne of David, reign over the house of David forever, and rule a kingdom which has no end (cf. Luke 1:31-33). The Hebrew Bible reveals that the Messiah would die for humanity's sin, be resurrected, and later establish an eternal kingdom of righteousness and peace (cf. Isa. 52:13-53:12; Ps. 16:10; Isa. 9:1-7).

Remember Peter's great confession of faith near that pagan worship center at Caesarea Philippi? Jesus asked the disciples, "Who do people say that the Son of Man is?" (Matt. 16:13) The disciples responded saying that there were many different interpretations of His Person circulating among the Jewish people. Jesus then asked them, "But who do *you* (i.e. you disciples) say that I am?" (v. 15) Peter answered for the rest, "You are the Christ, the Son of the living God" (Matt. 16:16).

The word "Christ" is essentially a title which means "anointed one." This title comes from the Hebrew Bible where the "anointed one" was a special designation for one who was set apart from others by the ritual of sacred anointing to represent God. Both kings and priests were anointed with olive oil in a ceremony which set them apart to represent God and serve God's people. There were many "anointed ones" in the history of God's people. But there was a very special "anointed one" who was promised by God to represent Him to humanity and to be the ultimate sacrifice for sins. John wants his readers to understand and embrace the truth that Jesus is the "anointed one," the Messiah promised by the Hebrew prophets.

The second term used in the New Testament to refer to Jesus is "Son of God." The seven miracles of John's Gospel are also designed to convince the readers that Jesus is the divine "Son of God." It is very significant that Jesus calls God His "Father" 106 times in John's Gospel and appeals to His "works" (ie., miracles) to prove His claims (John 5:36; 10:265,38; 14:11). Jesus told the Jews, "I and the Father are one" (10:30). The word "one" is neuter and suggests that the Father and Son are one divine essence. There are three Persons in the Trinity (better, *Tri-unity*), but only one God. Jesus and the Holy Spirit share in an essential unity with the Father. When Philip said, "Lord, show us the Father, and it is enough for us," Jesus responded with the words, "He who has seen Me has seen the Father" (14:8-9). Jesus claimed to be the divine Son of God! Even Jesus' enemies understood His claim to deity. They accused Him of "calling God His own Father, making Himself equal with God" (5:18).

Perhaps as a prospective disciple, you are evaluating for the first time the claims of Jesus. Perhaps like many people of the first century, you believe that He is a good man, or even a prophet. But do you believe that Jesus is who He claimed to be—the divine Messiah of Israel, the Son of God? You may be sincere in your religious convictions, but unless you believe that Jesus is the Son of God, like Charlie Brown, you will find that sincerity is not enough in the game of life.

The Result of Belief (20:31c)

Belief, John tells us, is not just an end in itself. Belief in the divine Messiah is designed to issue in *life*. "But these have been written that you may believe that Jesus is the Christ, the Son of God; and that believing you may have life in His name" (20:31). Since Jesus has life in Himself, He has the authority to give life to whom He wishes (5:21, 26). The "life" which results from belief includes both a *quantitative* and a *qualitative* aspect.

The "life" which results from believing in Jesus is often described as "eternal" (3:16). It is a quantity of life in that it precludes perishing. Jesus says about His own, "And I give eternal life to them, and they shall never perish; and no one shall snatch them out of My hand" (10:28). The word "life" if frequently used by John to refer to a believer's heavenly destiny (3:36; 5:29; 12:25). It is "life without end" in the resurrection body through which believers will enjoy heaven's eternal bliss.

Eternal life, however, is not just "pie in the sky." There is a present, qualitative aspect to the "life" which results from believing in Christ. Jesus said, "I have come that they might have life, and might have it abundantly" (10:10b). Christ, who is the life (11:25); 14:6), grants life as a *present* possession to those who believe in Him. "Truly, truly, I say to you, he who hears My word, and believes Him who sent Me, has eternal life, and does not come into judgment, but has passed out of death into life" (5:24). The essence of this present tense aspect of eternal life is an ever increasing personal knowledge of God the Father as made known through Jesus the Son (17:3).

Eternal life is like an insurance policy which combines "whole life" and "term" insurance. Term insurance builds no equity. It is only good for the future. Payment of the policy comes at the death of the insured. Whole life insurance, on the other hand, builds equity which can be drawn upon for a down payment on a house or the purchase of a car. It is your money, so you can use it during your life—as long as you continue to make payments on your policy. Like a combined whole life and term policy, eternal provides a present benefit along with a future blessing. Believers enjoy abundant life in Christ now (John 10:10) while anticipating an unending life in the future (John 3:16). Followers of Jesus don't have to wait until they die to enjoy eternal life. It is a present possession as well as a future hope!

What is Your Decision?

What is your decision as a prospective disciple? Do you believe what the Apostle John said about Jesus? Have you trusted in Him as the divine Son of God and Savior of the World? Are you ready to place your confidence in Rabbi Jesus, coming under His teaching and authority? Are you ready to be a Jesus follower? The discipleship instructions of Jesus will have little impact on your life if you are unwilling to acknowledge Him as your teacher and enter His apprenticeship.

A story tells about a Saxon king who put down a rebellion in a distant province of his kingdom. When the insurrection had been quelled, the king placed a burning candle over the archway of his castle and announced that all who had rebelled would be spared if they surrendered their weapons and took an oath of loyalty to the king. The king offered the rebels his clemency and mercy, but the offer was limited to the life of the burning candle!

Every great offer in life has its expiration date. There is a limited period in which to make use of the opportunity. This is true of the greatest offer ever made to humanity— the offer of eternal life through Messiah Jesus, God's Son. If you have not already done so, welcome and receive God's offer of salvation while the candle of your life yet burns. Not only will you receive God's gift of eternal life, but Jesus' final discipleship instructions in the Upper Room Discourse will take on new and greater significance for you as a follower of the Master Disciple Maker.

Study and Review Questions

1. Write a summary statement about the life of the Apostle John. What life-changing experiences can you identify in his life?
2. What is a biblical miracle? How is the biblical use of the term "sign" distinguished from common usages of the word "miracle"?
3. What are the signs or miracles in John's Gospel designed to accomplish in the minds and hearts of prospective disciples?
4. Define "belief" as it is used in John's Gospel. How is biblical "belief" distinguished from "intellectual assent?"
5. What does the designation "Christ" mean? How does this term relate to the Jewish expectation of a coming Messiah?
6. Did Jesus ever claim to be divine? How did He prove His claim?
7. Define the concept of "eternal life." Is eternal life simply a provision for the future? If we have it now, is it something we could ever lose?
8. How would you use John's Gospel to present the message of salvation to someone who is not yet a follower of Jesus? What key verses would you use in your presentation?
9. Write a paragraph explaining how John 20:30-31 relates to your personal spiritual journey. Does this

text describe where you are spiritually *or* where you want to be? Are you ready to become a disciple of Jesus?

Chapter 2

A Disciple's Ministry

John 13:1-20

A witty preacher once said, "Selfishness is that detestable vice which no one will forgive in others, and no one is without in himself." The truth of this statement was evidenced during my student days at the University of Oregon. Before the advent of computer registration, students had to be on campus three days before the beginning of the quarter in order to register for classes. There were always a limited number of openings in the more popular classes; so it was essential to be at the proper classroom to sign up at your "priority hour." During that hour, for instance, students with the last names beginning with the letters L, M, and N had preference.

Registration for classes in the English Literature Department was held in MacArthur Court, the home court of the University of Oregon's basketball team, the "Fighting Ducks." I'll never forget taking my place on a bench as a freshman and watching a swarm of students from the earlier priority hour descend upon the court to register for the classes they had to take. After I waited for three hours on the bleachers, the signal was given and the rush was on! It was every student for him or herself. They pushed, shoved, and shouted. Some students registered for the class they wanted and dashed off to the next building to wait for their priority hour for another class. Others were in tears, having been shut out of classes they needed to take. Many students, grimly resigned to their fate, began to rework their schedules to accommodate other classes.

Fortunately, for incoming freshmen, the University of Oregon has switched to on-line computer registration. The lines are gone, as is the pushing, shoving, and crowding. But the selfishness which motivated it all is still there. It is present in the heart of every entering freshman. You see this selfishness when people want to be the first to enter a store for a black Friday sale. You see it when traveling and everyone wants to get off the airplane to make their connection. Some wait patiently, but other travelers crowd ahead.

It seems that the selfishness which permeates our society often finds its way into our own lives. Perhaps you have said, "I sure didn't get anything out of that church service today." "When is the new pastor going to call on *me*?" There are many who call themselves disciples and attend church, participating in its activities, only for what they can get out of it for themselves.

The first portion of Jesus' words to His disciples in the Upper Room deals with this crucial issue. Here Jesus shows His followers that discipleship is about serving others, not ourselves.

Every follower of Jesus is called by God to the ministry of serving others—motivated out of one's love for Christ.

The Circumstances of the Disciples (13:1-3)

John 13:1-3 reveals the circumstances of Jesus' final instructions to His disciples before His death. Earlier in the day, Peter and John had made preparations for the Passover supper (Luke 22:7-8), one of the three great pilgrim feasts celebrated annually in Jerusalem (cf. Deut. 16:16). The Passover meal was to be eaten at night within the city. Since none of the disciples resided in Jerusalem, they observed the Passover meal in a large, furnished upper room which was graciously made available to them, possibly by Mary, the mother of John Mark (Luke 22:9-12; Acts 12:12).

It was the night before His crucifixion. Although Jesus had repeatedly predicted His death, the twelve disciples gathered in the Upper Room did not fully understand what He had meant. Jesus, however, knew what His death would mean and the Father's exact timetable for this culmination of His ministry. John 13:1-3 says that on the night before His death, Jesus was conscious of three things.

First, Jesus was conscious of His hour (13:1). He knew that the hour for His impending death and departure from the world had come (12:23). This knowledge prompted Jesus to show His love for His own through a powerful illustration. The phrase, "He loved them to the end," does not mean simply to the end of His life. The "end" suggests the idea of "uttermost degree." The love of Jesus for His own is set in stark contrast with the selfishness of Judas, who had already arranged for the

Lord's betrayal (13:2). Yet the hatred and hostility of the world never overcame Jesus' love for His own.

Second, Jesus was conscious of His authority (13:3a). He knew that the Father had given all things into His hands—the authority to give life and to execute judgment (5:25-27). He knew He had the authority to call on more than twelve legions of angels for His deliverance (Matt. 26:53), but Jesus yielded that prerogative.

Third, Jesus was conscious of His commission (John 13:3b). He knew that His commission was from His Heavenly Father and that He would return to God with His mission accomplished.

Why does John focus our attention on the fact that Jesus was conscious of His hour, His authority, and His commission? John is about to describe a situation in which Jesus takes a very lowly position, but the apostle does not want us to lose sight of the fact that the highest possible place is Christ's by divine right.

The Example of Humble Service (13:4-11)

The background of the foot-washing described by the apostle in John 13:4-11 is found in Luke 22:24-27. You would think that on such a special occasion as a Passover with Jesus, the disciples would be kind and thoughtful of one another. But Luke tells us that the disciples were quarreling! On their way to the Upper Room the disciples were disputing over who was going to be the greatest in the coming Messianic kingdom! Each of the disciples was probably thinking the words that Cassius Clay (aka, Mohammed Ali) used to shout when he was the world heavyweight boxing champion, "I am the greatest!"

Jesus had taught His disciples that greatness in the kingdom comes through serving others (Matt. 20:26-27), but they had apparently not learned the lesson. Now, just as the Passover was about to begin, Jesus proceeded to give the Twelve Apostles an unforgettable illustration of this important truth.

In the land of Israel, the roads are dusty and feet get dirty. Although guests would bathe before a social gathering like Passover, after a walk across town their feet would be dirty again. My wife Nancy and I became well aware of this when we studied in Jerusalem at the Jerusalem University College (formerly the Institute of Holy Land Studies) for a summer. Although we would shower after an all-day field trip to some ancient site, after our evening walks through the dusty streets of the Old City, we found it necessary to wash our feet before slipping into bed. Nancy insisted on this ritual in order to keep our clean sheets free from the dust and dirt of the Jerusalem streets. In ancient times, a basin of water and several towels were customarily placed at the door of a home for washing. The task of washing guests' feet was generally assigned to a household servant.

A basin of water and towel had been left in the Upper Room for the disciples' use, but not one of the Twelve had stooped to the task of washing the others' feet. They were too busy arguing over who would be the greatest in the kingdom. Christ's humble example rebuked their haughty attitudes. Jesus was about to give His disciples a lesson they would never forget.

Laying aside His outer robe, Jesus wrapped Himself with a large towel, poured water into a basin, and began washing the disciples' feet. Matthew, silently watching this supreme example of Jesus' condescension, would later recall and record His words, "The Son of Man did not come to be served, but to serve" (Matt. 20:28). After encouraging an attitude of humility among the believers at Philippi, Paul would later describe how Jesus "humbled Himself by becoming obedient to the point of death, even death on a cross" (Phil. 2:8).

There must have been a quiet atmosphere in the Upper Room that night as the disciples watched the Master assuming the role of a servant. The conversation probably stopped as Jesus went from one disciple to another, washing and drying their feet. Then Peter, the disciple with the foot-shaped mouth, spoke up and challenged the procedure. He protested with the question, "Lord, do You wash my feet?" (John 13:6). It was not the time or the place for foot-washing since the supper had already begun. Nor was Jesus the one to be doing such a humble task! Jesus explained that only "hereafter" would they understand the significance of His actions (13:7). This indefinite time reference could refer to the future illumination of His teaching by the Holy Spirit (14:26; 16:13) or to the explanation Jesus would give, beginning in verse 12. The context would suggest the latter interpretation.

Peter continued to vigorously protest what he viewed as inappropriate procedure, "Never shall You wash my feet!" (13:8a). Expositors debate the meaning of Jesus' response, "If I do not wash you, you have no part with Me" (13:8b). In the context, "wash" must refer to the washing of feet. Jesus came to earth to serve (Mark 10:45), and Peter's refusal of that service was in essence a rejection of Christ's person. Jesus was saying, "Peter, if you don't receive My ministry, of which this foot washing is an example, then you are guilty of rejecting My person and work, and cannot be My disciple." Peter responded, "If that's the case, Lord, then give me a bath!" Jesus patiently reminded Peter that one who has already bathed needs only to wash his feet.

At this point in the conversation, Jesus elevates the conversation from the realm of the physical foot washing to spiritual cleansing (John 13:10b). The disciples were "clean"—spiritually pure and faithful (cf. 15:3), but Judas was the one exception since he had plotted to betray Jesus. John confirms this interpretation in the next verse. Jesus said, "Not all of you are clean." And in verse 11 the Apostle John explains, "For He knew the one who was betraying Him, for this reason He said, 'Not all of you are clean.'"

Many expositors take John 13:10 to be teaching the need for confession and cleansing from sin. The word "bathed" is seen as referring to the "washing of regeneration (Titus 3:5), and the word "washed" as pointing to the cleansing described in 1 John 1:9. Accordingly, Jesus would be understood to be teaching, "If you have been *bathed* (regenerated), then you only need to be *washed* (cleansed from sin through confession)." While the bathing and washing imagery could well illustrate the teaching of Titus 3:5 and 1 John 1:9, I believe that the need for cleansing from sin is not the point of verse 10. All too often the primary point of this passage is missed by those who seek some deeper spiritual meaning.

Two important rules for interpreting Scripture guide our consideration of this text. *First*, don't add to the interpretation if an explanation is provided in the context. *Second*, prefer the clear and simple interpretation over one that is more complex.

With the help of these guiding principles, I find four reasons to steer clear of the view that Jesus is referring in verse 10 to cleansing from sin. (1) Jesus was dealing with the problem of humility, not sin. (2) In His explanation, Jesus makes no reference to the washing of regeneration or the cleansing from sin. (3) Jesus commanded His disciples to follow His example (vv. 14-15), and they have no authority to cleanse others from sin. (4) Judas' feet were apparently washed along with the other disciples, yet he was unsaved. There was no cleansing from the defilement of sin in his case. Teaching the need for the washing of regeneration and cleansing from the defilement of sin is essential! But those truths are taught elsewhere in Scripture. And you don't want to miss the great truth that Jesus taught uniquely here.

The Instructions Concerning Ministry (13:12-20)

If we look for the explanation Jesus gives the disciples after the foot washing, and prefer the clear meaning over one that appears obscure, we discover a very significant lesson for the followers of Jesus. We learn from Jesus' explanation of the foot washing the kind of humble service to others that should characterize His disciples. What is emphasized by Jesus is the *attitude* of service to be demonstrated by disciples in daily living. John 13:12-20 answers the question, "What is a disciple's ministry all about?"

First, a disciple's ministry is *service*. After washing the disciple's feet, Jesus returned to the table and began to probe the disciples, "Do you know what I have done for to you?" (13:12). Jesus went on to explain that since He, the Lord, acted as a servant, then certainly the disciples should be seeking to serve others rather than arguing over their positions in the future kingdom.

Regarding the foot-washing Jesus declares, "For I gave you an example that you also should do as I did to you" (13:15). The word "example" (*hupodeigma*) literally means "pattern." In the foot-washing, Jesus gave the disciples something to pattern their lives after. Jesus did not use the Greek word *tupos* which would refer to an act that the disciples were to exactly replicate. In other words, He is not saying, "Wash feet." Rather, Jesus is saying, "Be a servant. Don't fuss over your positions in the future kingdom. Keep busy here and now by focusing on your ministry of serving."

Second, a disciple's ministry is service *for others*. Note Jesus' words in verse 14, "wash one another's feet." A disciple's ministry is serving *others,* not him or herself. It is through your service that Jesus will meet others' needs. Many cathedrals in Europe suffered damage as a result of bombing raids during World War II. The explosion of a bomb in one great cathedral blew the hands off a statue of Christ. Though the cathedral was repaired, the statue of Christ stands there today with its hands missing. But an inscription on the pedestal reads, "Christ hath no hands but yours." Jesus depends on faithful Christians to reach out for Him and touch the lives of those who hurt.

Third, a disciple's ministry is *humble* service. In verse 16, Jesus reminds His disciples of their status as "slaves" or "servants." The slave is not greater than his master. The point is that if Jesus, the Master, serves, how much more willing ought the disciples to serve. A disciple's ministry is a humble service. Disciples should not seek the honor that is due Jesus, but rather serve with that attitude which was so well exemplified by John the Baptizer (John 3:26-30).

When John's followers were leaving him to follow Jesus, John might have become jealous and self-seeking. But instead, he likened himself to a friend of a bridegroom. He did not want to stand in the limelight that was reserved for Jesus alone. As a humble servant, John declared, "He must increase, but I must decrease" (3:30). John the baptizer modeled a humble attitude in serving others that the Lord Jesus would have us follow.

Finally, a disciple's ministry is a service which *brings blessing*. There is a blessing for the one who follows Jesus' example of humble service in ministering to others (13:17). The word "blessed" literally means "happy." It is great to know the teachings of Jesus about serving others, but there is no blessing, fulfillment, or real happiness if these truths are not personally applied. The great violinist Niccolo' Paganini (1782-1840) willed his marvelous violin to the city of Genoa on the condition that it must never again be played. The wood of such an instrument, while used and handled, wears only slightly, but set aside it begins to decay. Paganini's lovely toned violin has today become worm-eaten and useless except as a relic. Today it serves as a solemn reminder of the absence of blessing on a life withdrawn from service to others. A person's unwillingness to serve may soon destroy his or her capacity for usefulness.

Now you might be saying, "I'm chomping at the bit to begin! How shall I serve others? What specifically should I do? Well, step one would be to begin using your spiritual gift(s). A "spiritual gift" is simply a God-given ability for service. All believers have one or more of these divine enablements (cf. 1 Cor. 12:7-11; Rom. 12:6-8). The Apostle Peter writes, "As each one has received a special gift, employ it in serving one another, as good stewards of the manifold grace of God" (1 Pet. 4:10).

You may be wondering, "What is my spiritual gift?" Well, don't lose sleep trying to figure it out. Simply ask yourself three simple questions: (1) "What do I enjoy doing?" (2) "What am I doing that the Lord seems to be blessing?" (3) "What do others commend me for doing well?" Chances are that you are already using your spiritual gift. If you are enjoying a ministry that the Lord is blessing and others are appreciating, keep up the good work!

Step two in becoming a servant would be to begin applying the "one another" passages of the New Testament. For an exciting and stimulating study, look up the words "one another" in a Bible concordance. Here are a few references for starters: Romans 12:10; 15:7; Galatians 6:2; Ephesians 4:32; Hebrews 10:24; 1 Peter 4:9; 1 John 3:11. In a great variety of ways, Jesus' disciples minister to *one another*.

A third step in becoming a servant is simply to focus on people rather than things. When you see people, you will see that they have needs. Perhaps you are the instrument through which Jesus will meet some of those needs. Jesus can use you to meet the needs of others if you are willing and available. In days of ancient Israel, God needed someone to preach to the disobedient people. Isaiah stepped up and said, "Here am I. Send me!" (Isa. 6:8).

Before concluding our consideration of a Christian's ministry, let's answer the question: What could motivate Jesus' disciples to follow His example, taking a basin and towel and washing someone's feet? People are motivated by different things—money, recognition, appreciation, enjoyment, and love.

While attending the University of Oregon, I spent several summers working at the Eugene Fruit Growers Association cannery. I addition to my other duties, I served on the cannery clean-up crew. We worked in rubber suits and sprayed down the canning machinery with a mixture of scalding water and steam. Only one thing kept me on that job—the promise of a fat paycheck! Yet I was once motivated by financial interests to give a series of messages in a church. It was a small church, but I assumed that the honorarium for four messages would amount to about what I could make helping paint a small house—my other alternative for a short-term job. Since I'd rather preach than paint, I took the preaching opportunity. To my disappointment, I received no check from the church. But through that experience, the Lord taught me an important lesson. Jesus' disciples must not let money motivate their ministry. If they do, they will most certainly be disappointed. On other occasions, I have served others out of a desire for recognition and approval. This too has proved unfruitful. What, then, will motivate a disciple to serve others when there is no financial remuneration, no recognition, and no appreciation? Jesus gives the answer in John 21:15-17. A disciple's motivation for ministry must be his or her *love* for Jesus.

John 21:15-17 does not deal with Peter's restoration to fellowship after his denial, for Jesus had already met with Peter privately and probably dealt with his denial at that time (Luke 24:34; 1 Cor. 15:5). Here in John 21 Jesus deals with Peter's responsibility as a leader and instructs him concerning his ministry as a disciple and *motivation for service.*

It is debated whether John intended of us to make a distinction between the two words for "love" in this passage, or whether he simply used the variation as a stylistic device and was just asking the same question three times. With the majority of expositors, I believe that a distinction is being made.

The word used by Jesus in John 21:15 is *agapao.* This may be defined as volitional love which can be commanded. It seeks the ultimate good of the one loved, even to the point of personal sacrifice (cf. Eph. 5:2). This *agapao* love may be thought of as "sacrificial commitment."

The word used by Peter in responding to Jesus is *phileo*. This word refers to an emotional love based on personal affection. It is related to the Greek word for "friend" and can be thought of as "affection." In verse 15, Jesus questions Peter about his sacrificial commitment, "Simon, son of John, do you love Me more than these?" Before Jesus' arrest, Peter had declared, "Even though all may fall away because of You, I will never fall away" (Matt. 26:33). Now Jesus questions him, "Peter, is your sacrificial commitment to Me really greater than that of the other disciples?" Jesus then gives Peter the responsibility of tending His lambs—caring for the needs of the young ones in the faith.

In verse 16, Jesus again questions Peter about his sacrificial commitment (*agape*), and Peter affirms his affection (*phileo*). The responsibility given Peter is to shepherd Christ's sheep—feed and guide the more mature believers. Finally, in verse 17, Jesus uses Peter's word and questions his affection. "Peter, is the affection (*phileo*) you profess genuine?" Peter assures Jesus that it is. He is given the responsibility to shepherd Christ's sheep, seeing to all the needs of Jesus' followers.

Jesus' conversation with Peter was designed to point the apostle to the key to faithful discipleship—a proper motivation for service. Peter's responsibility as a disciple was to feed and care for Jesus' followers. That's service for others. His motivation for this service would be his love for Jesus. Sacrificial commitment to Jesus would be essential to keeping Peter at the task of serving others.

The disciple's ministry is service for others, motivated out of love for Christ. Sacrificial love (*agape*) for Jesus is the only sufficient motivation to keep disciples faithfully serving others. If Peter is motivated by anything else, he will be disappointed, discouraged, and will give up, for the task is great. And this is true for *any* disciple.

Jesus concludes His conversation with Peter by warning him what serving others would ultimately cost him (21:18-19). Peter would die a martyr's death at Rome, under the Neronian persecution of A.D. 64. According to Origen, cited by Eusebius, Peter was crucified head down just outside the gates of the city (Eusebius, *Historia Ecclesiastica* 3:1). But Peter knew that his ministry as a disciple was *serving others*. And his love for Jesus kept him faithful to the task until death!

Study and Review Questions

1. Describe the setting for the Upper Room Discourse.

2. What does it mean that Jesus loved His disciples "to the end"? (13:1). How is Jesus' love for His own a key to our understanding of what should motivate a Christian's ministry?

3. What were the disciples discussing when Jesus took up the basin and town and began washing their feet? (Luke 22:24-27).

4. Why did Peter say to Jesus, "Never shall You wash my feet"? (13:8a).

5. How do you understand Jesus' words, "If I do not wash you, you have no part with Me"? (13:8b).

6. Does John 13:10 teach the need for confession and cleansing from sin? Explain your answer.

7. How does the word "example" (13:15) help us understand Jesus' instructions concerning the foot-washing? What does He mean, "You also ought to wash one another's feet"? (13:14).

8. One way to serve others is to use your spiritual gifts. What is a "spiritual gift"? How does one go about determining his or her gifts?

9. What motivates *you* to serve others? What does Jesus' conversation with Peter in John 21:15-17 teach disciples concerning motivation for serving others?

Chapter 3

A Disciple's Love

John 13:21-35

Benedict Arnold (1741-1801) was a Patriot officer who loyally and courageously served the cause of the American Revolution until 1779 when he shifted his allegiance to the British. In May 1778, Arnold joined George Washington at Valley Forge, and when the British evacuated Philadelphia, he was appointed military commander of the city. There he enjoyed Philadelphia's social life, moving among families of loyalist sympathies. Benedict Arnold had a passion for money, and needed lots of it to support his extravagant style of living. To raise extra money, he violated several state and military regulations but was soon discovered and denounced by Pennsylvania's Supreme Executive Council.

While his personal integrity was being called into question by some Americans, Benedict Arnold married Peggy Shippen, a young woman of loyalist sympathies. Then, in early May 1779, he began to supply the British with military intelligence and demanded money for his services. His motive for treason was personal rather than political. He had a lust for money and desired to avenge himself against those who had questioned his integrity. On July 15 of the following year, Arnold asked the British for 20,000 pounds for betraying his command of West Point. When his British contact was captured, Arnold knew that his treason would soon be exposed, and he escaped to England on a British ship. There he spent the rest of his life in obscurity, his name having become a synonym for treason among the American people.

Another name recognized as a synonym for treason by all the Christian world is Judas Iscariot, the disciple who betrayed Jesus for 30 pieces of silver. In this chapter, we will examine this ultimate act of betrayal. What motivated Judas? What could have counteracted such selfish ambition and hostility? How can Jesus' disciples be assured that they will not betray their Master as Judas did? What motivation is sufficient to keep disciples following in the footsteps of their Discipler?

The Identity of the Betrayer (13:21-30)

Little is known for certain about the early life of Judas. What kind of a home was he raised in? What was his father like? Was he raised in a single parent home? We may be able to identify his home town. The epithet "Iscariot" may be a Hellenized form of the Hebrew *ish Kerioth*, "man of Kerioth." If Judas came from the Judean city of Kerioth (about 14 miles south of Hebron), then he was the only one of the disciples who was not Galilean (cf. Acts 1:11). But another tantalizing possibility is that "Iscariot" is related to the Latin term *sicarius* used as the designation of a radical "Zealot," a member of that party of Jewish patriots who so zealously and violently opposed Roman rule in Judea. Members of the *sicarii* armed themselves with a *sica* or "dagger" which they concealed in their robes. At festivals and in crowded marketplaces, they would carry out assassinations of community leaders and public officials not sympathetic to their cause. We know that there was at least one Zealot among the disciples—Simon the Canaanean, or better, "Zealot" (Matt. 10:4; Mark 3:18). Was Judas a member of this extremist political group? There is no way of knowing for certain, but if he was, it would certainly help explain his dissatisfaction with Jesus' rather conciliatory approach in dealing with Judea's Roman rulers.

Like the other disciples, Judas probably joined Jesus' company of followers because he believed Jesus to be the promised Messiah and the One who would overthrow Roman's domination over Israel. While Jesus was indeed Israel's Messiah, He was teaching the disciples that He must die for the sins of the world before He could rule the nations. For the other disciples this truth was incomprehensible. To Judas, it was totally unacceptable.

Jesus had some important things to share with His disciples during the last hours before His arrest and crucifixion. But these words were meant only for His faithful followers. Jesus would have to dismiss Judas, the betrayer, from the Upper Room so that He could spend His last hours with His committed disciples.

Troubled in spirit, Jesus solemnly announced, "Truly, truly, I say to you, that one of you will betray Me" (13:21). Looking around at one another, the disciples simply could not comprehend who would commit such treason. Certainly Jesus had enemies, but would one of His own disciples turn against Him?

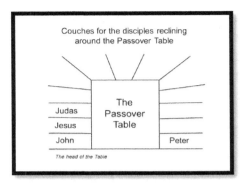

Couches for the disciples reclining around the Passover Table

Judas

Jesus

John

The Passover Table

Peter

The head of the Table

An understanding of the cultural situation at the Last Supper will help us to interpret verse 23 and better understand the dynamics of the narrative that follows. In the first century it was customary, when eating, to recline on couches around a low banquet table. Resting on their left elbows, diners reached for food and ate with their right hands. It seems to have been the established rule that the principal guest—in this case Jesus—reclined at the head of the table. We know from the Gospel narrative that John the Apostle was at a place of honor to the right of Jesus, and Judas was at a place of honor to His left. Peter was on a couch directly opposite John and was thus able to ask across the table who the betrayer was (13:24). This diagram illustrates the arrangement of the disciples around the Passover table.

A superficial reading of verse 23 might lead us to believe that one of the disciples was using Jesus' chest as a pillow while reclining around the Passover table. This is not how the author intended his account to be understood. The disciple "whom Jesus loved" is identified in John 21:20,24 as the author of the Gospel—the Apostle John. Rather than John reclining *on* Jesus, the Greek word for "on" (*en*) suggests simply that John was in the *sphere* of Jesus' chest. John was just to the right of Jesus, and both were propped up on their left elbows. In this position, John was able to lean back toward Jesus' chest and speak to

Him over his right shoulder. Even around a crowded banquet table, the two were able to have a private conversation about the betrayal.

Peter, sitting across the table from John, asked his fellow disciple to find out from Jesus who the betrayer was (13:24). Leaning back toward Jesus, John asked over his right shoulder, "Lord, who is it?" (v. 25). Jesus responded by telling John that He would identify the betrayer by giving him the morsel after dipping it (13:26). According to Jewish tradition recorded in the Haggadah (the *telling* of the Passover story), the morsel would have consisted of some bitter herbs and *haroseth* (a mixture of chopped apples, nuts, spices and wine) on a piece of unleavened (pita) bread. Offering the morsel at a Passover was an expression of friendship and love. It signified special respect and manifested good will. Jesus may have been making one final, gracious appeal to Judas to repent. But the heart of Judas was hardened, and he was unresponsive to Jesus' expression of unrelenting love. Judas took the morsel from Jesus, identifying himself to John (and probably also to Peter) as the betrayer.

What motivated Judas to betray the One who was offering him love and friendship? I believe that there were two significant factors which led to this disciple's betrayal of Jesus. The first was the influence of the Evil One whom we know as "Satan." John tells us that the devil himself put the plan to betray Jesus into the heart of Judas (13:2). Later during the Passover supper, after he had taken the morsel from Jesus, Satan actually entered into Judas (13:27). This appears to be a case of what is commonly known as "demon possession." But this terminology is somewhat misleading since there is no concept of "possession." The Greek word (*daimonizomai*) means "to demonize" (Matt 15:22) which suggests the idea of demon *influence* rather than demon *possession*. Satan apparently *demonized* Judas to accomplish the evil task of betraying his Master, Jesus. This was another of Satan's attempts to frustrate God's plans and purposes for Israel's Messiah.

The second factor which led Judas to betray Jesus was his lust for money. Judas had undoubtedly hoped to receive some material reward for following Jesus. But now he realized that his rabbi was going to die and there would be no possibility of enrichment in the long anticipated kingdom. John tells us that Judas had been pilfering the disciples' community purse (12:6), but he must have expected to make his "big haul" in the messianic kingdom. Concluding that Jesus was not going to take the throne of Israel, Judas sought to salvage whatever material gain he could out of his investment in this relationship. Matthew 26:14-16 tells of the financial arrangements Judas made with the Jewish leaders. He agreed to betray Jesus for a mere 30 pieces of silver—the price of a gored slave in ancient Israel (Exod. 21:32).

Knowing full well Judas' plans to betray Him, Jesus spoke to His unfaithful disciple, "What you do, do quickly" (John 13:27). There must have been sadness in His voice as Jesus spoke these words. He was not above being hurt and disappointed by betrayal. None of the other disciples gathered around the Passover table understood the purpose of Jesus' instructions to Judas. Some thought that Jesus wanted Judas to purchase something for the feast. Others assumed that Judas had been instructed to give alms to the poor as was customary at such a celebration as Passover (12:29). None of the disciples reclining at the Passover table realized that the words of Jesus set into motion a chain of events which would ultimately lead to His death on a Roman cross.

After taking the morsel, Judas immediately left the Upper Room. Observing this decisive moment in the life of Judas, John records, "and it was night" (13:30). Of course it was night! It was Passover evening! But is there more implied by John's comment than that the sun had set and that it was dark outside. I suggest that John is using the word "night" in a figurative sense (cf. 9:4; 11:10). John is telling us of the spiritual darkness in the soul of a disciple who had separated himself from Jesus—the Light of the world. There was a deep, spiritual darkness in the heart of Judas as he left the Upper Room to carry out his plans to betray Jesus.

There is an important lesson for followers of Jesus from life of Judas. Although he had an association with Jesus, Judas had set his affections on the things of this world, laying up his treasure on earth rather than in heaven. His priorities were all mixed up! And this can happen to anyone of us! Sometimes disciples, like Judas, allow their priorities to become confused with the result that they devote excessive amounts of time and energy in the pursuit of the dollar and passing pleasures rather than focusing their attention on Jesus. This cautionary comment doesn't mean that we should neglect our jobs or financial responsibilities. That too would be out of order (cf. 2 Thess. 3:10-12). Rather, we must guard against majoring on the relatively insignificant things of life, allowing them to distance us from Jesus. Disciples of Jesus must view life's priorities from a divine perspective, focusing on that which will count for eternity.

In the Berlin Art Gallery hangs a painting by the great German painter Adolf Menzel (1815-1905). The painting is only partially finished. It was intended to portray Frederick the Great speaking with some of his generals. Menzel carefully painted all the generals and background but he left the king until last. He was able to sketch the outline of Frederick the Great in charcoal, but died before he was able to finish the painting in oil.[4] Like Menzel, many Christians come to the end of their lives without ever having put Christ into His proper place—on center stage, not standing in the wings.

The Mark of a Disciple (13:31-35)

Judas' betrayal of Jesus was a sin against love. Instead of demonstrating love and devotion for the one who had extended to him friendship and grace, self-seeking Judas responded with deception and hostility. The betrayal of Christ by Judas stands as the ultimate treason. Judas not only sinned against the Savior's love, but hypocritically betrayed the Master with a kiss---a phony demonstration of affection. It is in the context of unbelieving Judas' sin

---

[4]To see the painting, go to http://www.fineart-china.com/upload1/file-admin/images/new12/Adolph%20von%20Menzel-248664.jpg

against love that Jesus reveals the mark of true and faithful disciples.

Because the departure of Judas from the Upper Room began a sequence of events which would eventuate in Jesus' glorification through His crucifixion and death, Jesus said to His faithful disciples, "Now is the Son of Man glorified, and God is glorified in Him" (13:31). Verse 32 reveals that as the Father would be glorified by the Son through His passion, so the Father would "immediately" glorify the Son through His resurrection. In this context, the word "immediately" would mean "after a short time," and alludes to the three days between Jesus' death and resurrection.

In verse 33, Jesus again announces His imminent departure from the earth and speaks of the separation from His beloved disciples which would result from His return to the Father in heaven. Jesus had spoken of this departure to the Jews earlier at the Feast of Tabernacles (7:33-34), but now He repeats this announcement for the benefit of the disciples. The statement, "Where I am going, you cannot come," raised some key questions in the minds of the eleven disciples remaining with Jesus in the Upper Room—questions which He would respond to in the dialogue which follows (13:36-14:25).

Before dealing with His disciples' questions, Jesus provides in verse 34 the key to counteracting the kind of selfishness and lack of love demonstrated by the actions of Judas. Speaking to the eleven remaining with Him in the Upper Room, Jesus said, "A new commandment I give to you, that you love one another, even as I have loved you, that you also love one another." The word

Jesus used for "love" is *agapao* and refers to a volitional love which can be commanded. This particular Greek word does not refer to an emotional attachment or a personal affection, but rather to a "sacrificial commitment." This "agape" love is an unconditional love which seeks the ultimate good of the other person—even to the point of personal sacrifice.

Jesus calls His command" a new commandment." But the command itself was not new. As far back as the time of Moses, God had instructed His people, "You shall love your neighbor as yourself" (Lev. 19:18). What was new about the "new commandment"? The new aspect of Christ's command to love one another is the *measure* of the love involved. Jesus commanded us to love one another "as I have loved you." How did Jesus love His own? John tells us that He loved His disciples "to the end" or better, "to the uttermost" (John 13:1). Jesus loved His disciples (and us) to the point of sacrificing His life (10:11; 15:12-13).

Paul encourages the same kind of sacrificial commitment in Ephesians 5:1-2 where he writes, "Therefore be imitators of God, as beloved children; and walk in love, just as Christ also loved you, and gave Himself up for us, an offering and a sacrifice to God as a fragrant aroma."

Jesus points out in verse 35 that "agape" love—sacrificial commitment for one another—is to be the distinguishing mark of His followers. Through the centuries people have used many different symbols to show that they are Christians—the sign of the fish, the emblem of a cross, a PTL (*Praise the Lord*) button, and now in the 21st century a Christian tattoo! But there is one universal mark that is to characterize Jesus' followers throughout the history of the church. That mark is "agape" love. Such sacrificial commitment to one another will identify Christ's disciples to all the world.

Note in verse 35 that an "if" is involved. The new commandment can be violated. Believers can sin against love even as Judas did. If, on the other hand, the command is followed, those who obey will wear the badge that Jesus gave. In his insightful little book, *The Mark of the Christian*, Francis Schaeffer comments with reference to the "if" found in John 13:35. He writes, "The point is that it is possible to be a Christian without showing the mark, but if we expect non-Christians to know that we are Christians, we must show the mark" (Inter-Varsity Press, 1970, p. 8).

How can this "agape" love be made visible in your life and mine? I suggest several ways. You may have some suggestions to add to the list.

First, love says, "I'm sorry." The classic film, *Love Story* (starring Ali MacGraw and Ryan O'Neal) popularized the catchphrase, "Love means never having to say you're sorry." But in contradiction to these words, the Bible reveals that love says, "I was wrong; I *am* sorry." James encourages believers to confess their sins to one another (James 5:16). A sincere apology not only becomes an antidote for bitterness, but also mends and strengthens relationships (cf. Matt. 5:23-24). I recall some time ago hearing that something untrue was being said about me by a seminary colleague. When I traced the story to its source, I confronted the offender with the sin of speaking about a brother falsely. Needless to say, I was steaming! But that Christian brother took my anger away when he looked me in the eye and said, "I'm sorry. I have been a Christian long enough to know better than to do something like that. Please forgive me." Whew! His gracious words of apology quenched my anger and restored our relationship. I have the utmost respect for a person who will admit his or her error and say, "I'm sorry." That is a manifestation of "agape" love—genuine sacrificial commitment.

Second, love manifests a forgiving spirit. Love forgives others even when they refuse to recognize their wrong. Paul says in Ephesians 4:32, "And be kind to one another, tenderhearted, forgiving each other, just as God in Christ also has forgiven you." Such a forgiving spirit registers an attitude of love toward others—the mark of a disciple. My son, John, was just three when I made the terrible mistake of disciplining him for something he did not do. I jumped to conclusions and disciplined him when he was not at fault. Knowing what I had to do, I looked him in the eye and told him that I was wrong and was sorry. I asked for his forgiveness. With tears still on his cheeks, that little boy put his arms around my neck and whispered, "I forgive you, Daddy." Now that's *agape* love!

Third, love sacrifices for others. Love is not just a banner, but rather the basis for practical, sacrificial service to others (cf. John 15:12-13). How long has it been since we really sacrificed to serve others in our families or in our churches? All too often we think of the family and even our church as a place to have our needs met—a place to be ministered to. That, however, is not love, for love sacrifices to serve others. Every church needs workers who are willing not only to help but also to make personal sacrifices of time and energy to serve others as teachers, youth sponsors, deacons, elders, or trustees. When you are asked to serve, give the request your prayerful consideration; count the cost; and then if God is leading you, accept the opportunity, for love *sacrifices* for others.

Perhaps the Apostle John had the new commandment in mind when he penned the words, "Beloved, let us love one another, for love is from God; and everyone who loves is born of God and knows God. The one who does not love does not known God, for God is love" (1 John 4:7-8). While hatred and hostility characterize the unbelieving world, "agape" love is the mark of a true disciple of Jesus.

Study and Review Questions

1. What do we know about the early life of Judas Iscariot? Does the epithet "Iscariot" shed any light on this question?
2. Describe the situation around the Passover table in which Jesus made known to Peter and John the identity of His betrayer.
3. What does John mean when he says that there was a disciple "reclining" on Jesus' breast? Who is the "disciple whom Jesus loved"? (John 13:23).
4. What motivated Judas to betray Jesus? How might a disciple betray Jesus today? How can this sin of betrayal be avoided?
5. How is the "immediately" of John 13:32 to be interpreted? When and how would the Father glorify the Son?

6. What kind of love does Jesus refer to in his "new commandment"? (13:34).
7. What is "new" about the new commandment that Jesus gave His disciples?
8. Offer some suggestions as to how the "mark of the disciple" might be displayed in the lives of Jesus' disciples today. Select one which you would like to begin displaying in your life this week.

Chapter 4

A Disciple's Destiny

John 13:36-14:6

I will never forget the phone call I received on the evening of April 15, 1972. I was typing a paper for a Hebrew language class which I was taking as a student at Western Seminary when the phone rang. I recognized my dad's voice and knew by the tone that something was dreadfully wrong. There was a long pause. Then Dad breathed the name of my younger brother, "Otis." Deep inside I feared the worst. I asked my Dad, "Is he gone"?

That Saturday morning my brother Otis and his friends had traveled to Mt. Bachelor, where they had enjoyed a beautiful day of spring skiing. After a great day on the slopes, Otis and his friends left the Mt. Bachelor parking lot about 4 o'clock for the 30-mile drive back to Bend, Oregon where they planned to spend the night. Suddenly, about ten miles from Bend they heard a loud bang. A blow-out! When the tire went flat, the car swerved to the left over the center line. As the young driver tried to compensate for the swerve, the little Volkswagen rolled to the left, over and over and over until it came to a rest right side up on the shoulder of the highway. Dazed from the impact, Otis' friend Bruce looked about the shattered car. Everyone was moving and there appeared to be no serious injuries. But where was Otis? Climbing out of the car, Bruce found Otis pinned underneath it!

Otis was rushed by ambulance to the Bend hospital, but doctors there were unable to tend to his severe injuries. The ambulance continued on to Eugene and arrived late Saturday evening. But Otis did not. Somewhere between Bend and Eugene, beneath the slopes of the beautiful Cascade mountains, Otis left his earthly body and entered the presence of Jesus whom he had trusted as his Savior (cf. 2 Cor. 5:8).

My brother's death has caused me to think a great deal about the subject of heaven. I am sure that every reader of this book has experienced the earthly loss of a friend or family member. If that person was a believer in the Lord Jesus, we can be assured that he or she is in heaven. But perhaps you have wondered as a disciple, "What is heaven like?" "When will we see our departed loved one again?" Jesus wanted His disciples to understand their heavenly destiny. In this chapter, we want to consider Jesus' answers to the disciples' questions about their heavenly destiny and their eternal home.

The Destination of Jesus (John 13:36-14:2)

In John 13:36-14:6, Jesus answers two important questions for the disciples. Jesus had just spoken of His departure. He said, "Little children, I am with you a little while longer. You will seek me; and as I said to the Jews, now I also say to you, 'where I am going, you cannot come'" (13:33). Apparently Peter did not completely understand this reference to Jesus' death and wanted further information. Picking up on the word "where," Peter asked the Master, "Lord, where are You going?" (13:36). Jesus responded, "Where I go, you cannot follow Me now; but you shall follow later" (13:36). Peter, who was determined to remain with Jesus whatever the cost (cf. Matt. 26:31-33), pressed Jesus for an explanation. "Lord, why can I not follow You right now?" Then he added the stirring promise, "I will lay down my life for You" (John 13:37).

I believe that Peter meant what he said. Later that night in the Garden of Gethsemane, Peter took up arms to defend Jesus to the death from those who came to arrest Him (18:10-11). Only Jesus' intervention prevented Peter from entering into armed combat with the Roman soldiers and the arresting officers there in the garden.

Peter seems to have had greater confidence in the steadfastness of his commitment than Jesus did. Peter must have been shocked to hear Jesus' words, "Will you lay down your life for me? Truly, truly, I say to you, a rooster will not crow until you deny Me three times." This sober announcement appears to have quieted Peter, for we don't hear from him again until Jesus' arrest in the Garden of Gethsemane (18:10).

Jesus' announcement of His departure (13:33) and prediction of Peter's denial (13:38) brought an atmosphere of gloom to disciples gathered in the Upper Room. Seeing the discouragement and despair in the eyes of His disciples, Jesus immediately dealt with this and answered Peter's earlier question. He commanded the disciples to *stop* letting their hearts be troubled (14:1). The second half of verse 1 can be translated in four different ways: (1) Believe in God, believe also in Me; (2) You are believing in God; you are also believing in Me; (3) Believe in God, you are also believing in Me; and (4) You are believing in God, believe also in Me. The thrust of the command is probably, "Keep on believing in God and in Me, His son." In other words, "Don't be discouraged! Keep the faith!" Continued trust in the Father and Son is set forth by Jesus as a divine antidote to discouragement and despair. If you find yourself discouraged, this prescription is relevant and applicable for you today.

John 14:2 contains the long-awaited answer to Peter's question, "Lord, where are You going?" Jesus explained, "In My Father's house are many dwelling places; if it were not so, I would have told you; for I go to prepare a place for you." Where is the "Father's house"? Remember the instruction of Jesus concerning prayer in Matthew 6:9? The disciples were taught to pray, "Our Father who is in heaven." The Father's house is in *heaven*! Jesus was departing from this earth so that He could prepare a residence in heaven for His people who would follow Him there.

The Description of Heaven (Revelation 21:9-22:5)

What will heaven be like? John 14:2 in the King James Version suggests that heaven will be a land of many "mansions." Actually, the word translated "mansions" literally read "abodes" and could better be translated "apartments." Now I believe they will be *nice* apartments. Jesus is there in heaven right now preparing them for us. I guarantee that you won't be disappointed in these eternal accommodations Jesus is preparing for His people!

Nowhere in Scripture do we find the complete details of what heaven will be like, but in Revelation 21:9-22:5 the curtain is drawn back to give us a glimpse of heaven—a foretaste of the glory that is to come. As Paul told the Corinthian believers, "Things which eye has not seen and ear has not heard, and which have not entered the heart of man, all that God has prepared for those who love Him" (1 Cor. 2:9; cf. Isa. 64:4).

In Revelation 21, the Apostle John is given a vision of the New Jerusalem. The fact that the New Jerusalem is referred to as a "bride" and "the wife of the Lamb" (Rev. 21:2,9) suggests that it be identified as heaven, the eternal residence of the body of Christ. This would be in keeping with the "bride" and "bridegroom" imagery used elsewhere in Scripture to describe the relationship between Christ and His church (cf. Eph. 5:22-32; 2 Cor. 11:2; Rev. 19:7).

Though John sees the city through a vision, there is every indication that it is a *literal* city. It has a wall (21:12), gates (21:12), measurable dimensions (21:16-17), streets (22:2), plants (22:2), and people (22:3). The New Jerusalem is also a *large* city. The dazzling city will measure 1,500 miles square and 1,500 miles high (21:16)! Perhaps instead of being a cube, it will be more like a pyramid in structure with private dwellings on various levels. The point is that there will be no housing shortage in heaven. There will be plenty of room for all who have believed in Jesus! Finally, the New Jerusalem is a *splendid* city (21:11). Its brilliance will make the most beautiful earthly place look drab! I remember visiting a fine crystal shop in Victoria, British Columbia. Its walls were paneled with mirrors, and its shelves were filled with clear, cut glass. The shop literally sparkled! It was beautiful indeed, but heaven will be even more splendid. The city won't be made of concrete and asphalt, but of jasper, pure gold, and precious stones (21:18-21). You may live in a humble home now, but in heaven you will dwell in kingly splendor!

John goes on to describe the kind of life disciples will enjoy in the New Jerusalem (21:22-22:5). No worship center will be found there, for the inhabitants will have direct access to God the Father and Christ the Lamb (21:22). The city will need no street lights, sun, moon, or stars, for it will be illuminated by the glory of God (21:23-24). This does not mean that natural light sources will not exist, but that they won't be necessary for light within the city. The gates of the New Jerusalem will never be closed, for neither Satan and his demons nor other enemies of God can threaten the disciples there (21:25-26; cf. 20:10,15). The New Jerusalem won't have a crime problem, for its citizens will be the redeemed whose names are written in the Lamb's Book of Life (21:27). Because it is a city where there is no sin, its trees and plants won't be subject to the curse which resulted from the Fall and will bear their fruit year round (22:1-3a). The citizens of heaven won't forever pluck harps, but they will serve the Father and Son (22:3b, 5) and share in Christ's reign over the universe (cf. 2 Tim. 2:12). Not only will they serve God, but they will also enjoy intimate fellowship with Him. They shall see His face (22:4). Heaven, then, is a beautiful place where believers will enjoy fellowship with Jesus (22:4), rest (14:13), joy (21:4), service (22:3), and worship (19:1; 7:9-12) for all eternity. What an abundant eternal life awaits those who have trusted in the Lord Jesus Christ!

The Reunion with Christ (John 14:3)

Jesus goes on in the Upper Room Discourse to assure His disciples that His departure will not be permanent. "And if I go and prepare a place for you, I will come again, and receive you to Myself; that where I am, there you may be also" (14:3). This is a clear reference to Christ's return for the church prior to the terrible judgments which will be poured out on the earth during the Tribulation (cf. Rev. 6-19).

It is important to distinguish between the *Rapture*—the blessed hope of Christ imminent (at any moment) return for His church—and the *Second Coming* when Jesus returns to the earth to judge His enemies and establish His kingdom. While not all my friends make this distinction, I am persuaded by Scripture that Jesus will come first for His saints (the Rapture) and then, after the seven-year Tribulation period, will come with His angels to set up His messianic (millennial) kingdom (Rev. 19:11-20:4). While the Second Coming is to be heralded by many signs (Matt. 24:3-30), the Rapture is an event which is unannounced and could occur at any time.

There are two main lines of reasoning that lead me to the "pretribulation" Rapture position. First is my understanding of the concept of "wrath" which appears to be the major characteristic of the Tribulation period. During the Tribulation, the people on the earth will say to the mountains and rocks, "Fall on us and hide us from the presence of Him who sits on the throne, and from the wrath of the Lamb; for the great day of their wrath has come; and who is able to stand" (Rev. 6:16-17)? Bearing this in mind, we note that the Thessalonian believers were encouraged by Paul to look expectantly for the coming of Jesus "who delivers us from the wrath to come" (1 Thess. 1:10). Later he points out to the Thessalonians that "God has not destined us for wrath, but for obtaining salvation through our Lord Jesus Christ" (5:9). The "salvation" refers in this context not to the salvation of souls, but to "physical deliverance" as the same word is used in Acts 7:25. Paul is saying that God has not appointed believers for the wrath of the Tribulation, but for physical deliverance from it through Christ's coming for His people at the Rapture.

My second reason for believing that the church will be removed to heaven before the Tribulation is based on 2 Thessalonians 2:3. The church at Thessalonica was going through such severe trials that some believers actually thought they were going through the Tribulation. Paul points out that two things have to take place before the Tribulation begins. The first is the "apostasy." The Greek word used here, *apostasia*, is derived from a verb meaning "to depart from" (*aphistemi*). According to its most basic root meaning, "apostasy" could be translated "departure." In fact, this is a definition listed in Liddell and Scott's *Greek-English Lexicon* (Oxford: At the Clarendon Press, 1889, p. 107). While this word can be used metaphorically of a departure from doctrine (cf. Acts 21:21), the *context* of 2 Thess. 2:3 would indicate that Paul is referring to the "departure" of the church. Notice in 2 Thessalonians 2:1 that Paul is writing regarding the coming of the Lord Jesus and particularly that aspect of the event which relates to "our gathering together to Him"—a clear reference to the Rapture (cf. 1 Thess. 4:17). Writing to a church that was going through severe persecution and suffering, Paul assures them that they were not enduring Tribulation sufferings because the departure has not yet occurred.

The second event which must take place before the Tribulation begins is the appearance of the "man of lawlessness" (2 Thess. 2:3), the "little horn" of Daniel 7:8, the so-called *Antichrist* of the end time (cf. Dan. 9:27). To the persecuted believers at Thessalonica, Paul says, "This is not the Tribulation because the church has not been raptured and the Antichrist has not been revealed."

Some have wondered if the believers' "blessed hope" (Titus 2:13) of Christ's imminent return for His church is a practical or worthwhile doctrine to study and embrace. It is amazing to me that virtually every time we have a reference to this doctrine in Scripture, there is some mention of how it applies to the Christian life!

67

The believer's blessed hope is first of all an encouraging hope (John 14:3). When the disciples were discouraged by the prospect of His departure, Jesus encouraged them with the promise of His return.

Second, the believer's blessed hope is a comforting hope (1 Thess. 4:13-18). After outlining the program of the Rapture for the Thessalonian believers, Paul said, "Therefore comfort one another with these words." Are you mourning the loss of a loved one in Christ? The blessed reunion you look for will take place at the moment of Christ's return! At the Rapture the dead in Christ will be raised first, and then we who are alive will be caught up together with them in the clouds to meet the Lord in the air (4:17). Then we will live forever with our loved ones and with Jesus.

Third, the believer's blessed hope is a motivating hope (1 Cor. 15:50-58). Paul concludes his discussion of the Resurrection by showing that it is absolutely necessary that the resurrection body be obtained either through death or translation at the Rapture. For Paul this doctrine was not merely academic, but practical. Confident that their labor is not fruitless, believers are exhorted to be steadfast in their commitment to Christ and diligent in their tireless service for Him (1 Cor. 15:58).

Finally, the believer's blessed hop is a purifying hope (1 John 3:2-3). Writing about Christ's future appearing, John says, "And everyone who has this hope fixed on Him purifies himself, just as He is pure" (3:3). Those who have their hope resting on the prospect of Christ's imminent return for His church keep themselves pure in anticipation of that blessed event. I remember attending a wedding on a rainy spring day, and the walkway between the parking lot and the church was covered with puddles. The groom was waiting inside when the bride arrived in her beautiful white wedding dress. You can imagine how carefully she made her way up that walkway to the church. He bridegroom was waiting, and she didn't want to meet him with her wedding dress wet and soiled from the puddles. Likewise, no believer would want to be found in a compromising situation or soiled by the pollution of this world's system when Christ comes.

The Way to Heaven (John 14:4-6)

Having answered Peter's question, "Where are You going?" Jesus remarked, "And you know the way where I am going" (14:4). Peter's theology of heaven had been a little shaky, but Jesus suggests that at least the disciples knew the *way* to get there! But Thomas was perplexed. He still did not understand clearly about heaven, and most certainly he did not know the way (14:5). Jesus did not get out a map of the universe to show Thomas how to get to heaven. He simply identified Himself as the way—the only way of access to heaven. Jesus said, "I am the way, the truth, and the life; no one comes to the Father, but through Me" (14:6). Only through Jesus and His sacrifice for sins on the cross can anyone gain entrance into heaven.

Notice that Jesus did not say, "I am one of the many ways to heaven," but rather, "I am *the* way! *No one* comes to the Father, but through Me." Jesus is quite narrow and exclusive on this point. There are many who say that it doesn't really matter what religion you choose—just so you are sincere. One of the main tenants of the Baha'i faith is the essential unity of all religions. It is the old "all roads lead to Rome" philosophy. This is one of Satan's most popular lies. In the Old Testament there was just one entrance into the tabernacle and only one way into the temple. There was only one way into the sheepfold, and Jesus claimed to be the "door of the sheep" (10:7). He said, "If anyone enters through Me, he shall be saved" (10:9). Paul writes that "there is one God, and one Mediator also between God and men, the man Christ Jesus" (1 Tim. 2:5). There is just *one* way, and Jesus is *the* way.

Jesus also claimed to be "the truth." The Person of Christ is the essence of truth. He is the very embodiment of God's reliable revelation. His mission was to bear witness to the saving truth of His deity and messianship! Over the entrance to the library at my alma mater, the University of Oregon, are inscribed the words, "And you shall know the truth, and the truth shall make you free" (8:32). Thousands of university students have walked through the library doors in search of knowledge, but have never come to a knowledge of *the* truth. Ultimate truth is found not in books, but in a Person. Truth is found in Jesus. To know Him is to know the truth.

In addition to being "the way" and "the truth," Jesus also claimed to be "the life." Since He has "life in Himself" (5:26), Jesus has the power and authority to give life to whom He wishes (5:21). Consoling Martha over the death of her brother Lazarus, Jesus declared, "I am the resurrection and the life; he who believes in Me shall live even if he dies" (11:25). Then to prove the truth of His claim, Jesus called Lazarus forth from the grave! The resurrection of Lazarus authenticates Christ's claim to be the life. Those who believe in Jesus will, like Lazarus, *live* even if their earthly life should end before Christ returns for His church.

Jesus is the way—without whom there is no going. He is the truth—without whom there is no knowing. He is the life—without whom there is no living. How, then, do you get to heaven? Through Christ! Precisely, (1) recognize that you have personally fallen short of God's high and holy standard, (2) realize that Jesus, God's Son, paid your debt by His death on the cross, and (3) receive Jesus as your personal Savior, trusting Him for deliverance from the penalty of your sins. Concerning the assurance believers enjoy, the Apostle John writes, "These things I have written to you who believe in the name of the Son of God, in order that you may know that you have eternal life" (1 John 5:13).

Someone might be saying, "But how can God forgive *all my* sins? Consider the story of the Russian Czar Nicholas (1796-1855) who used to visit his army late at night. One night he decided to visit an officer whom he had known from his youth. The officer had embezzled funds from the government expecting to someday pay it back, but the debt became too great. He was about to take his own life when he fell asleep at his desk with the records of his embezzlement before him. On the open record book, he had written, "So great a debt, who can pay?" While the soldier was sleeping, Nicholas entered his tent and understood what had happened. Out of mercy and pity, he signed his name to the records: "Nicholas." The offer later awoke in his tent and realized what had happened. He didn't take his life, for Nicholas had paid his debt! Similarly, Jesus has written His name across our sins. He has paid our debt. Our ticket to heaven has been purchased with His own precious blood. Disciples of Jesus have a heavenly destiny. They look expectantly for Jesus' return to take His people to their eternal home— the celestial city. At the end of the Book of Revelation, John Himself speaks and promises, "Yes, I am coming quickly" (Rev. 22:20). Within our hearts we say with John, "Amen. Come, Lord Jesus."

Study and Review Questions

1. Why do you suppose that Jesus did not immediately answer Peter's question, "Lord, where are You going?" (John 13:36).
2. Was Peter serious when he told Jesus, "I will lay down my life for You"? (13:37).
3. How did Jesus deal with the discouragement which came over the apostles as they learned of His impending departure?
4. What indications are there that the New Jerusalem of Revelation 21 ought to be identified with heaven?
5. What is heaven like? Describe the place in your own words.
6. What distinction is made between the Rapture and the Second Coming?
7. What is the next major prophetic event in God's program for the church? How do you know?

8. Is the doctrine of Jesus' return for the church of any practical value for Christians today? What difference should the "blessed hope" make in the life of a disciple?
9. How would you explain to an unbeliever that Jesus is the way to heaven?

Chapter 5

A Disciple's Power through Prayer

John 14:7-15

Theodosius I was the emperor of Rome (A.D. 379-395) during the great controversy between the followers of Arius and the disciples of Athanasius over the deity of Christ. Athanasius was a clear-minded, skilled theologian who affirmed the full deity of Jesus the Son and His equality with God the Father. While in his 20s, Athanasius wrote his treatise, *On the Incarnation of the Word of God*, in which he expounded the eternal sonship of the divine Logos—Jesus. On the other hand, Arius, who was a presbyter in charge of a church in Alexandria, taught that Jesus was not the eternal Son of God, but a subordinate being, neither fully God nor fully man, but something in between. Such a view undermined the biblical teaching on the deity of Jesus.

The Emperor Theodosius was apparently sympathetic toward the unorthodox views of Arius and was about to decide the matter at a meeting of the bishops at Constantinople (381). During the opening ceremony, the bishops individually entered the emperor's court, acknowledged both the emperor and his son, and then departed. All was going well until Amphilochius, bishop of Iconium, entered the court. He acknowledged only the emperor and ignored the presence of his son, Arcadius. When commanded to acknowledge the emperor's son,

Amphilochius simply said, "Save you, child." The enraged emperor ordered Amphilochius to acknowledge his son or leave the court. Amphilochius turned to leave, but before exiting he stopped dramatically and addressed the emperor, "You want me to acknowledge your son. But are you willing to acknowledge God's Son?"

The issue at stake at the Council of Constantinople was the deity of Christ. Was He equal with the Father? Or was He a lesser, created being? What should disciples believe about Jesus? What does the Bible teach? In this chapter, we want to consider the *person* of Christ and His relationship with the Father. We also want to focus on the *power* available to disciples through prayer in Jesus' name.

The Person of Christ (John 14:7-11)

In John 14:7, Jesus leads the disciples into the next question: "If you had known Me, you would have known My Father also; from now on you know Him, and have seen Him." The conditional construction of verse 7, "If you had known Me," implies that up to this time the disciples had not really known Jesus in an intimate, personal way, and hence had not known the Father. But from this point on, things would be different. Through Jesus, the disciples would know and experience a relationship with God the Father. As the Apostle John stated in the prologue of his Gospel, "No man has seen God at any time; the only begotten God who is in the bosom of the Father, He has explained Him" (1:18).

In response to Jesus' words concerning the Father, Philip speaks up and requests, "Lord, show us the Father, and it is enough for us" (14:8). Have you too had a secret longing see God the Father with your own eyes and thereby be assured of His existence? What would it be like to see God? Jesus explains to His disciples in the Upper Room that it has *already* happened!

Jesus responded to Philip's request with a gentle rebuke, "Have I been so long with you, and yet you have not come to know Me, Philip?" (14:9). Though Philip had been with Jesus since the beginning of His public ministry (1:44-45), he had not yet grasped the full significance of His person. Then, Jesus made a simple but profound statement regarding His relationship with the Father, "He who has seen Me has seen the Father; how do you say, 'Show us the Father'?" (14:9). Earlier in His ministry, Jesus had declared, "I and the Father are one" (10:30). While there are three Persons in the Godhead—the Father, Son, and Holy Spirit—there is only one God. Jesus is pointing to the fact that He shares one divine essence with the Father. A disciple who worships God cannot ignore His son!

The Apostle Paul wrote in Colossians 1:15 that Jesus is the "image" (*eikon*) of the invisible God. The Greek word *eikon* is used by Jesus in Matthew 22:20 to refer to the Roman emperor's image on a coin. The word points to the fact that Jesus is the One on whom the Father has "engraved" His divine image.

On a shelf in my office I have a proof coin given to me by my father-in-law. It is an Eisenhower silver dollar minted in 1971, the year of my marriage to his daughter

Nancy. A proof coin is unique, having on its surface the first impression made by a new coin stamp. The image of such a coin is perfect—without flaw. The coins made later by the coin stamp have slight imperfections due to wear and oxide. Jesus is like a proof coin—the perfect impression of the Father.

Jesus encourages Philip and the other disciples to believe that He shares an essential unity with the Father (John 14:10-11). He points to the fact that the Father and Son *indwell* each other. Twice Jesus declares, "I am in the Father, and the Father is in Me." Each is "in" the other. This points to the truth of the Trinity that while there is just one God—one divine essence—there are three Persons in the Godhead. The Father, Son, and Holy Spirit all share in this divine essence. The mutual indwelling of the Father and Son was something that the Jews should have recognized (10:38) based on Jesus' miracles. Certainly, Philip, one of the Twelve, should have known this truth.

Jesus appeals to His *words* and His *works* as evidences of His union with the Father. Jesus' words do not originate with Himself (14:10,24; 7:17). The message He speaks comes from God and is delivered at the Father's initiative. Jesus views Himself as the channel for revelation from the Father, and His message ("words") points to the fact of His union with the Godhead. His "works" or miracles are the second evidence Jesus offers for His union with the Father (cf. 5:36; 10:38). Jesus declared to the Jews at the Feast of Dedication just four months before His crucifixion, "The works that I do in My Father's name, these bear witness of Me" (10:25).

Nicodemus properly responded to these works when he told Jesus, "Rabbi, we know that you have come from God as a teacher; for no one can do these signs that You do unless God is with him" (3:2). The miracles were not designed to entertain the crowds but to lead them to the truth of Christ's person. Jesus is convinced that an appreciation for His authenticating miracles will lead people to believe in the truth of His mutually indwelling relationship with God the Father (10:38).

The deity of Christ, which was the central issue at the Council of Constantinople, is also a key issue today. The Jehovah's Witnesses teach that Jesus was not equal to God but was a created being. According to their doctrine, when Jesus lived in heaven He was known as the Angel Michael. When He came to earth, He lost His angelic nature and became a mere man. Since He was only a man when He died on the cross, His death is not sufficient to atone for the sins of the world. A works system of salvation must then be instituted. The Christian Science sect also denies the deity of Christ. Following the teachings of Mary Baker Eddy, Christian Scientists acclaim Jesus as a great teacher but do not believe that He is divine. The Unitarians, along with many liberal protestant groups, also deny the deity of Jesus today.

I am glad to say that the Roman Emperor Theodosius I, in part due to the challenge by Amphilochius, became persuaded of the full deity of Jesus. He drove the Arians, who had rejected the doctrine of Christ's deity, out of the churches at Constantinople and declared in July of the year 381 that all the Christian churches must be given bishops who believed in the equal deity of the Father,

Son, and Holy Spirit. The three are One--separate but equally divine persons—within the *tri-unity* of God.

The Power through Prayer (14:12-14)

A man once regarded as the greatest preacher in the English speaking world, Dr. John Henry Jowett (1863-1923), once said, "I'd rather teach one man to pray than ten men to preach!" As I have studied the lives of men and women whom God has used in remarkable ways, I have found that they have at least one thing in common. They placed a high value and priority on prayer.

In my own personal devotional life, I have found that prayer is one of the most rewarding Christian disciplines, yet one of the most difficult to develop and maintain. There is a reason for this. One of Satan's chief concerns is to keep Christians from praying. He fears nothing from prayerless studies, prayerless work, prayerless religion. He laughs at our labors and mocks our witness, but trembles when we pray!

The Power

John 14:12-24 tells of Jesus sharing with His disciples one of the keys to effectual prayer. The solemn "truly, truly" of verse 12 underlines the importance of the statement that Jesus makes about prayer. He declared to the disciples, "I say to you, he who believes in Me, the works that I do shall he do also; and greater works than these shall he do; because I go to the Father."

What are these "greater works" which the disciples would be able to accomplish? Was Jesus declaring that the disciples would do *more* miracles than He did during His earthly ministry? This does not appear to be the case. There are thirty-six specifically recorded miracles of Jesus found in the Gospels, and only twenty specifically recorded miracles in Acts.

Did Jesus mean the disciples would do *greater* miracles than He? Probably not, since the miracles of the apostles were primarily miracles of healing. No apostle in the Book of Acts ever walked on water, stilled a storm, or fed 5,000.

Do the greater works refer to *more conversions* through the ministries of the disciples? Possibly. It may be that the greater works were those of evangelizing and discipling which resulted in innumerable conversions and tremendous church growth throughout the Mediterranean world.

There is one more view that should be considered. The context points to the possibility that the "greater works" mentioned by Jesus are those things which would be accomplished by *prayer* in His name. Jesus said that the greater works would be possible "because I go to the Father" (14:12). The writer of Hebrews encourages believers to bring their requests before God's throne of grace because they have a sympathetic High Priest—Jesus—who ever lives to make intercession for them (Heb. 4:14-16; 7:24-25).

The Privilege

In John 14:13, Jesus reveals a new truth to the disciples. In Matthew 6:9, He taught them to pray to the "Father" in heaven. Now Jesus informs them that prayer will be answered when they ask the Father "in His name." Jesus said, "And whatever you ask in My name, that will I do" (John 14:13; cf. 15:16; 16:23-24,26). What does it mean to pray "in Jesus' name"? All too often this becomes merely a traditional formula we attach to our prayers with little thought or reflection. This borders on the "meaningless repetition" which Jesus Himself condemned (Matt. 6:7).

Believers have the privilege of praying "in Jesus' name." We may bring requests before the Father on the basis of Jesus' person and works—all that He is and has done for us. What specifically does it mean to pray in Jesus' name?

(1) To pray in Jesus' name is to pray in accordance with all that His name literally means and stands for—salvation! Praying in Jesus name means that we recognize Him as the divine Son of God and Savior who died for the sins of the world.

(2) To pray in Jesus' name means an appeal to the Father on the basis of Jesus' merits and influence as our great High Priest and intercessor (Heb. 4:14-16; 7:25).

(3) To pray in Jesus' name means to pray a prayer consistent with His holy and righteous character (cf. Dan. 9:16, 18-19).

(4) To pray in Jesus' name is to request the Father for what Jesus would want. It means praying according to God's will (1 John 5:14). When we pray "in Jesus name" we are saying, "I ask this, Father, because it is what I believe Jesus wants for me."

(5) To pray in Jesus' name means to seek that which would glorify the Father (John 14:13). It means praying that God's plans and purposes will be accomplished for His ultimate glory (17:4).

(6) To pray in Jesus' name is like signing His name to our prayer. The Father will answer the prayer because it is like a request from His dear Son.

(7) To pray in Jesus' name is to pray believing that God will grant the request for Jesus' sake (Matt. 21:22). It means to pray with bold faith in God's power and willingness to honor His Son by answering our prayer.

Praying "in Jesus' name" does not happen merely by concluding the prayer with the traditional formula, "in Jesus' name, Amen." Since we rarely give thoughtful consideration to the meaning of the words, "in Jesus' name," it may be well to avoid using the formula and replace it with some other expression acknowledging the person of Christ as the basis for our prayer.

To remind myself and those I lead of the significance of praying in Jesus' name, I sometimes begin my prayers by simply acknowledging to the Father that it is on the basis of the merits and influence of the Son that I present my petition. Having made my request, I simply conclude with "Amen."

Sometimes I will just breathe a brief prayer acknowledging in my heart that it is because of Jesus that I can approach the Father. Jesus was not encouraging

His disciples to adopt a new formula but rather to appropriate a totally new concept of prayer.

The Promise

Jesus promised His disciples that He would personally carry out the requests made to the Father in His name. "And whatever you ask in My name, that I will do.... If you ask Me anything in My name, I will do it" (John 14:13-14). Notice that Jesus uses the words "whatever" and "anything." He puts no restrictions on this promise. There is no limit to the power and potential available to a believer through prayer in Jesus' name. Praying in Jesus' name is the key to successful prayer. Now, don't misunderstand! God may not always answer our prayer in the way we want or expect. Sometimes God's answer is, "Wait." And sometimes He answers, "No." But we can be assured that when our requests are according to God's will, He will give us our requests for Jesus' sake.

Purpose

The purpose of answered prayer is to glorify the Father. Jesus said, "That I will do, that the Father may be glorified in the Son" (14:13). God is glorified when His reputation is enhanced and magnified. Here is one key to knowing whether or not your request is according to God's will (1 John 5:14). Ask yourself, "If my prayer is answered, will the Father be glorified? Will the answer to my prayer enhance God's reputation?" If you can answer, "yes," it may well be a request that is according to God's will. Jesus desires to answer our prayers to bring the Father glory.

Can prayer be genuinely a *Christian* prayer if it does not conclude with the words, "in Jesus' name?" It is interesting to me that even in churches I attend or visit, the words "In Jesus' name," are sometimes omitted from the prayer. I recognize Jesus was not calling for a rigid formula to be legalistically attached to our prayers. But Jesus *did* give His disciples instruction on how to pray in a way that honors His name and secures a receptive hearing from God the Father. I sometimes paraphrase what it means to pray in Jesus' name. I will say something like, "I bring this prayer to you, Father, based on all that Jesus is and has done as my Savior and Lord. I believe that this prayer is in keeping with your will and the answer will bring glory to your name. Amen!"

Paul added some helpful instruction on prayer in his letter to the Thessalonians. He wrote, "Pray without ceasing" (1 Thess. 5:17). The word "unceasing" is used outside the Bible to refer to a "cough." When you cough, you don't cough all the time, but the *tendency* to cough is always there. So it is with "unceasing prayer." The tendency to pray is always there.

When disciples encounter a physical or spiritual need, their first response should be to bring the concern to the Lord as Peter did when he felt water seeping through his sandals and cried out, "Lord, save me!" (Matt. 14:30). Prayer is simply the spreading out of our helplessness and that of others, in the name of Jesus, before a loving Father, who knows and understands, who cares and answers. What a privilege it is to communicate with the Creator through prayer!

The Potential of Love (John 14:15)

John 14:15 introduces a thought which Jesus will pick up again later in this chapter (vv. 21-24). How do you show someone you love him or her? Husbands, how do you let your wife know that you love her? Now it is good to say, "I love you," but words alone are not always convincing. I can tell my wife Nancy that I love her and then walk away from a table full of dirty dishes, but those words will have a hollow ring. How much more meaningful and convincing would those words sound if I would tell her to take some personal time to read or relax while I clear the table and wash the dishes? Love is best demonstrated through actions. In verse 15, Jesus reveals that this principle has definite application in our relationship with Christ. Jesus told His disciples, "If you love Me, you will keep My commandments." The measure of a disciple's love for Christ is his or her obedience to His Word!

The word for love used in verse 15 is *agapao*. This Greek word refers not to an emotion or an affection, but rather to a sacrificial commitment. It is love measured by personal sacrifice. It is the love of John 3:16, "For God so loved the world, that He gave His only begotten Son." It is the love Paul wrote of in Ephesians 5:2, "And walk in love, just as Christ also loved you, and gave Himself up for us, an offering and sacrifice to God as a fragrant aroma."

Jesus is pointing out to His disciples that our relationship with Him involves ethical responsibilities. The one who truly loves Jesus will not just say it but will demonstrate it by his or her actions—by obedience. How consistently do we obey Christ's teachings? It is so easy to find excuses for our disobedience. We can appeal to the circumstances or situations which would appear to make obedience difficult or "impossible." A more "scholarly" approach is to explain this or that teaching away as pertaining to ancient culture and having no relevance or application for today. Sometimes we appeal to our intellect. We won't obey this teaching or command simply because it doesn't make good sense to us. We just don't understand the reason for it. But note carefully; the measure of our love for Christ is our obedience to His command, and obedience does not depend upon total comprehension of why He says what He does.

When my children were little, I warned them against crossing the busy street in front of our house without holding my hand. Not fully understanding the reason behind my request, my young son would clasp his *own* little hands together thinking this was sufficient. But holding his own hands together would not protect him from stepping in from of an oncoming car! He had to hold *my* hand. God's children must learn to obey Him even though we don't completely understand the reason why.

Your love for Jesus is measured by your obedience to His teaching. If Jesus had to give you an evaluation of your love for Him today on a scale of one to ten, what would be the measure of your love? Anything short of ten is disobedience and sin. To disobey Jesus' teaching is to demonstrate a lack of love for Him. Let's covenant together to move that "love quotient" closer to ten!

A story told by a missionary from the country of Zaire in Africa illustrates the blessings of obedience. In a garden behind the missionary's home, his small child was playing under a tree. Suddenly from the back porch his father shouted, "Philip, obey me instantly—get down on your stomach." The boy reacted at once, and his father continued, "Now crawl toward me quickly!" Again, the boy obeyed. Then his father said, "Now stand up and run to me." The boy reached his father's arms and turned to look back. Hanging from a branch over where the boy had been playing was a large, poisonous viper!

Are you always ready to obey the Lord, or do you ask why and demand an explanation? Or do you say, "I will obey, but after a while." Let's be disciples who, by our immediate and consistent obedience to God's Word, demonstrate our genuine love for Jesus.

Study and Review Questions

1. What did Philip ask of Jesus in John 14:8? What do you suppose led Philip to make such a request?
2. How does the Son reveal the Father? Are there other ways through which God the Father is revealed?
3. What evidence does Jesus appeal to in order to prove His union with the Father?
4. If you had the opportunity to prove the deity of Jesus in court, what arguments would you use?
5. What are the "greater works" which Jesus promised that His disciples would be able to accomplish? Explain your answer.
6. What does it mean to pray "in Jesus' name"? Explain this in a way that even a child could understand it.

7. Why is the obedience of a disciple so important to Jesus? What excuses do Christians sometimes offer to explain or justify their disobedience to Christ's commands?
8. How can you encourage "love-motivated obedience" in your own life and in the lives of other disciples of Jesus?

Chapter 6

A Disciple's Promises

John 14:16-31

Expounding eloquently on the importance of honesty and faithfulness to one's word, a preacher asked the rhetorical question, "When is a promise not a promise?" Under his breath a local politician muttered, "When it is a campaign promise!"

You have heard it said, "Promises are made to be broken." When was the last time you were the victim of a broken promise? Was it the last presidential campaign? Was it when your husband promised you the evening out, but broke the date because of a business engagement? Was it back in high school when your Dad promised you the keys to the family car to drive to the football game, but cancelled those plans when he saw your report card?

I must admit that I have broken a few promises too. I have canceled plans made with my family and heard those piercing words from my children, "But Dad, you promised!" I remember one summer when I had a reduced teaching load and promised my wife a free day each week for shopping or visiting friends. This would give her a good break from wiping noses and changing diapers. Although I was sincere in my promise, not long into the summer I found myself heavily involved in a writing project. I was "on a roll" and wanted to finish the project before the beginning of classes in the fall. The "free day" I had promised Nancy turned out to be a "free afternoon," part of which she spent taking our son to his swimming lesson at the YMCA!

John 14:16-31 records some promises Jesus made to His disciples. Unlike the promises of overly zealous politicians, fallible friends, and well-intended spouses, the promises made by Jesus are promises that He will keep! Jesus has both the will and the power to fulfill His promises—promises of a coming Helper, fellowship with the Godhead, and a legacy of peace. These are promises that disciples of Jesus must embrace daily!

The Promise of a Helper (14:16-17, 26)

John 14:16-17 tells of Jesus promising His disciples a "helper"—One who will serve as their able assistant for their life and ministry ahead. How encouraging to know that the followers of Jesus don't have to "go it alone!" We have a helper identified by Jesus as the "Holy Spirit" who came at Pentecost (Acts 2:1-4; 11:15) to empower and enable God's people.

John 14:16-17 is the first of a series of important references to the Holy Spirit in the Upper Room Discourse (cf. 14:26; 15:26; 16:7-15). Here, Jesus promises his followers the coming of a helper, the Holy Spirit. "And I will ask the Father, and He will give you another Helper, that He may be with you forever" (14:16). The Holy Spirit is revealed to be "another" (*allos*) Helper. The word "another" means "another of the same kind." In other words, the helper will be of the same character and quality as the divine Jesus Christ. This is in keeping with the clear teaching of Scripture that the Holy Spirit is deity and serves as the third person of the Trinity or better, *Tri-unity* (cf. Acts 5:3-4; Matt. 28:19; 2 Cor. 13:14). The Helper is promised to the disciples in light of Jesus' announced departure. Christ's ministry on earth was temporary—a mere three and a half years—but the Holy Spirit is sent "that He may be with you *forever.*"

The word "Helper" (*parakletos*) is a word that can be used in a legal sense of a friend of the accused—an advocate or counsel for the defense—who is called upon to speak on behalf of another. The word is used this way to refer to Jesus in 1 John 2:1. But the more common usage of the word is in the general sense of a "helper"—one called alongside to help or encourage. The picture presented by this word is that of a long battle involving troops who are weary and fatigued. But when news comes that the long-awaited reinforcements have arrived at the battlefield. Soon fresh troops will join them in the trenches to carry on the campaign. The Holy Spirit is that kind of "Helper"—a mighty reinforcement for battle-weary disciples.

The Holy Spirit is designated in John 14:17 as "the Spirit of truth" (cf. 15:26). He is characterized by the truth (14:6) and communicated the truth to others (16:13). He is One whom the unbelieving world will not receive because unbelievers do not know Him or understand His workings. The disciples, on the other hand, entered into a personal relationship with the Holy Spirit even as they did with Jesus. In verse 17 Jesus points to a change in the Holy Spirit's manner of working from the Old Covenant to the

New Covenant. Previously, the Holy Spirit had been *alongside* the disciples, but soon the relationship would be even more personal. The Holy Spirit "will be *in* you," not just alongside you, explained Jesus. This means that under the provisions of the New Covenant, the Holy Spirit will personally *indwell* each and every one of Jesus' disciples (cf. 1 Cor. 6:19; Rom. 8:9).

John 14:26 gives further insight into the ministry of the Holy Spirit. Jesus said, "But the Helper, the Holy Spirit, whom the Father will send in My name, He will teach you all things, and bring to your remembrance all that I said to you." Here the Helper promised by Jesus is specifically identified as the "Holy Spirit." As the third Person of the Trinity, the Helper is "holy"—set apart from all that is contrary to the righteous character and nature of God. The Helper is "spirit"—just as God is spirit (John 4:24). This does not mean that the Holy Spirit is any less a real person, for He possesses the characteristics of a person (intelligence, emotions, and will), acts like a person (Rom. 8:26), and is designated as a person (John 14:17, note the pronouns "Him" and "He"). The Holy Spirit, then, is a separate, spiritual Person. He is sent by the Father in the name of the Son—on the basis of the Son's merits, influence, and request (14:16).

One of the special helping ministries of the Spirit will be that of teaching. Jesus promised that the Holy Spirit would teach the disciples and cause them to recall the things He had told them. He elaborates on this ministry later in the discourse (16:12-15). The teaching ministry of the Holy Spirit is not limited to the apostles (1 John 2:27), but was especially for their benefit as authors of God's

Word. Through the power and ministry of the Spirit, Matthew and John were able to recall Christ's words and record them as Scripture.

The Helper promised by Christ came at Pentecost and now indwells all believers to assist them in Christian life and ministry. Even writing to the problem-plagued Corinthian believers Paul could say, "Or do you not know that your body is a temple of the Holy Spirit who is in you, whom you have from God?" (1 Cor. 6:19) The promise of a divine Helper is a promise Jesus kept. Have you been looking to the Holy Spirit to help you in your life and ministry? He is always there, ready to come alongside and encourage you!

The Promise of Fellowship (14:18-24)

The second great promise Jesus made to His disciples assures them of having the privilege of enjoying fellowship with Him and with the Father. What comes to your mind when you contemplate the word "fellowship"? Do you think of having dinner with Christian friends, singing as a congregation in church, or enjoying punch and cookies in the church fellowship hall? Actually, the word "fellowship" is derived from the Greek word *koinonia* and simply means "a sharing in common." The early church enjoyed fellowship. "And they were continually devoting themselves to the apostles' teaching and to fellowship (*koinonia*), to the breaking of bread and to prayer" (Acts 2:42). While a biblical concept of fellowship would include visiting and spending time with other disciples of Jesus, the word points primarily to a *participation* together in life and ministry. Paul thanked God for the Philippians' "participation (*koinonia*) in the Gospel" (Phil. 1:5). The Gospel and changed their lives, and they had joined with Paul in communicating that message to others.

One of the more memorable fellowship experiences I enjoyed during my student days at seminary was going street preaching with several other students. During the noon hour we would position ourselves on a strategic street corner and begin our "street meeting" by singing a few verses of the classic hymn, "At the Cross." Then each of us would have the opportunity to stand on a folding chair and preach God's plan of salvation to the people passing by. A few people would stop and listen before continuing on their way. I don't know if this is the most effective way to share the gospel, but I look back with fond memories on those times of fellowship in the ministry as we prayed, preached and proclaimed the truth of God's Word. As we ministered together, we experienced what Jesus promised His disciples—a sharing in spiritual life and ministry with the Triune God—Father, Son and Holy Spirit!

In John 14:18, Jesus picks up on the subject of His departure (13:33,36; 14:3) and assures the disciples of His return to them at His resurrection. "I will not leave you as orphans; I will come to you" (14:18). He promised to come to His disciples and fellowship with them during His forty-day post-resurrection ministry (cf. Acts 1:3). Only a short time remained before Jesus would suffer and die on the cross at Golgotha. But after three days He would be resurrected and the disciples would see Him again (14:19). Jesus goes on to say, "because I live, you shall live also" (v. 19). Paul elaborates further concerning the relationship between Christ's resurrection and the believers' future life in 1 Corinthians 15:20-22. Because of the solidarity between Christ and the believers, His resurrection must result in the believers' resurrection. In Adam all people die, while in Christ all believers are made alive—both spiritually (in life) and physically (at the resurrection). Jesus is the "first fruits" of the resurrection which all His disciples have a part.

The impact of Christ's resurrection is revealed in John 14:20. The resurrection of Jesus will convince the disciples of the unity of the Father and Son, and their (the disciples') intimate relationship with Christ as believers. The resurrection was the culminating factor in the disciples' faith. When John entered the empty tomb, "he saw, and believed" (20:8). Thomas saw the resurrected Lord and said, "My Lord and my God!" (20:28).

In John 14:21, Jesus develops the thought introduced in 14:15 that one's love for Christ will be demonstrated by obedience to His will. "He who has My commandments and keeps them, he it is who loves Me." It is not enough to have an intellectual understanding of Christ's commandments; they must be practiced in daily life. As James puts it, "doing" the Word, not merely "hearing" it, is what really counts with God (James 1:22-25). God views love as something communicated not by words but by deeds. The one who genuinely loves Jesus will obey His teachings.

In the latter half of John 14:21, Jesus goes on to reveal that the one who loves the Son will be loved by the Father. Jesus is not saying that the Father rewards with love those who love His Son. Rather, the Father is not indifferent to the manner in which people respond to His Son. I believe that most parents have a special appreciation for those who take an interest in their children. How do you respond to a Sunday School teacher or pastor who knows your child's name and takes an interest in their life and spiritual development? God the Father responds in a similar way to those who regard His Son. Not only will the Father love such a disciple, but Jesus will too.

In verse 21, Jesus also promises to "disclose" or reveal Himself in some special way to His disciples. This self-disclosure is left unexplained and provokes a question by the other Judas (not Iscariot, cf. Luke 6:16). He said to Jesus, "Lord, what then has happened that You are going to disclose Yourself to us, and not to the world?" (John 14:22). Judas was concerned over the prospect of Jesus' disclosure being private rather than public. Like his Jewish countrymen, and perhaps the other disciples, Judas expected the Messiah to appear in glory before the whole world, judge the Gentiles, and restore the kingdom to the Jews (cf. John 7:4; Dan. 7:13-14; Zech. 14:1-5). Jesus answers the question by pointing to the necessary prerequisites for the disclosure about which He speaks. Those who are characterized by *love* and *obedience* will be loved by God and enjoy a special fellowship with the Father and Son. "If anyone loves Me, he will keep My Word; and My father will love him, and We will come to him, and make Our abode with him" (John 14:23). The idea of God dwelling among His people was not unfamiliar to the Jews. He had done this on various occasions in the past (cf. Exod. 25:8; 29:45; Zech. 2:10). But the united dwelling of the Father and the Son in the disciples is a new concept! Jesus is teaching that the Father, Son, and Holy Spirit will dwell or abide in the lives of His faithful disciples.

Have you pondered the fact that those who love and obey Jesus partake in a unique fellowship with the Trinity—the Father, Son, and Holy Spirit? This is not the kind of fellowship associated with punch and cookies, but rather a fellowship associated with ministry. As servants of the New Covenant (2 Cor. 3:6), we fellowship with the Holy Spirit when we witness (cf. John 15:26-27). We fellowship with Jesus when we are carrying out His commission to make disciples (Matt. 28:19-20).

The Promise of Peace (14:25-31)

Chapter 14 of the Gospel of John closes with a renewed emphasis on Christ's departure and its consequences for the disciples. Since the disciples were troubled over the prospect of Jesus' impending departure (13:36; 14:1,5), He promised them His own peace to encourage their calmness and confidence in the struggles ahead. "Peace I leave with you; My peace I give to you; not as the world gives, do I give to you. Let not your heart be troubled, nor let it be fearful" (14:27). What was this legacy of peace that Jesus promised His disciples?

Was it peace among nations? The Society of International Law in London has confirmed that during the last 4,000 years there have been only 268 years of peace in spite of 8,000 peace treaties. In the last three centuries there have been 286 wars on the continent of Europe alone!

Was it peace in the cities that Jesus promised? Sadly, Detroit continues to be the number one most dangerous city in the United States with a violent crime rate of 2,137 for every 100,000 residents. In 2014, America had a violent crime rate of 365.5 per 100,000 residents with a murder rate of 4.5. St. Louis came in with the highest murder rate of nearly 50 murders for every 100,000 residents. And mass murders, like the 58 killed in Las Vegas and the 17 shot in a Florida high school, continue.

Well then, was the peace that Jesus promised a peace in our homes. The American Psychological Association reports that about 40 to 50 percent of married couples in the United States divorce. The divorce rate for subsequent marriages are even higher.

Peace? Where is that promise being fulfilled today? What did Jesus mean when He said, "Peace I leave with you; My peace I give to you"? A little background study on the word "peace" will help us answer that question.

The New Testament word for peace (*eirene*) has much the same meaning and usage as the Hebrew word for peace (*shalom*) which is used throughout the Hebrew Bible. The word "peace" was used in the biblical period as a greeting and a farewell. Jesus greeting His disciples after the Resurrection with the words, "Peace be with you" (20:19,21). Paul used this word in his epistles both as a greeting (Gal. 1:3) and a farewell (Eph. 6:23). The word "peace" is also used to describe harmonious relationships between people (Mark 9:50; Rom. 14:19) and between nations (Rev. 6:4).

In the Scriptures, the word "peace" also has messianic connotations. The Old Testament prophets anticipated a messianic age of peace. They recognized that the chaotic state of the world was the result of humanity's sin and knew that peace could come only as God's gift. They looked with anticipation to the peace which was to be a prominent feature of the messianic kingdom. Isaiah prophesied the advent of a "Prince of Peace" who would establish and preserve peace in the messianic age (Isa. 9:6). The prophets looked forward to peace—both national (Isa. 2:2-4; 11:6-9; Zech. 9:9-10) and individual (Isa. 32:17-18; 53:5; 54:13; 55:12) as a fruit of the messianic reign.

When Jesus wept over Jerusalem and declared, "If you had known in this day, even you, the things which make for peace" (Luke 19:42), He was referring to the establishment of the kingdom of peace anticipated by the prophets. But because of the rejection of Jesus by the Jewish nation, the kingdom had to be postponed. The New Testament reveals that the thousand year (Rev. 20:1-6) kingdom of peace will be established when Jesus returns and subjects all the enemies of truth and good under His sovereign rule.

The word "peace" is also used in the New Testament to describe the spiritual well-being of true believers. The Gospel message of salvation in Christ is essentially a message of peace between God and humanity. At the birth of Jesus, the angels announced, "On earth peace" (Luke 2:14). Christ Himself "preached peace" to both the

Jews and Gentiles (Eph. 2:17). He "made peace through the blood of His cross" (Col. 1:20); and "He Himself is our peace" (Eph. 2:14). Paul writes in Romans 5:1, "Therefore having been justified by faith, we have peace with God through our Lord Jesus Christ." Some texts indicate that a better rendering of this verse would be, "*Let us embrace* peace with God through our Lord Jesus Christ." Having been justified by faith, we are able to enjoy peace with God through the reconciling work of Jesus on the cross. Peace is actually the fruit of a relationship with God through Jesus Christ (Gal. 5:22).

What then, was the legacy of peace that Jesus promised His disciples in John 14:27? First, the peace Christ promised is a spiritual *peace with God.* This was the peace Jesus Himself enjoyed in perfect fellowship with the Father. He said, "My peace I give to you." The peace that Jesus enjoyed with the Father is made available to every believer today! Jesus prepared the way for peace with God by removing sin's enmity through His sacrificial death on the cross. This is what "reconciliation" is all about. Reconciliation by the death of Christ means that our state of alienation from God is changed so that we are now able to be saved (2 Cor. 5:19). When an individual believes and is justified ("declared righteous), peace with God is established (Rom. 5:1). Such peace with God is found *only* in Christ. Jesus said, "These things I have spoken to you, that in Me you may have peace" (John 16:33).

Many people are seeking peace today, but they want peace *without God.* They want instant peace just to get them through some rough circumstances. Several years ago I crashed on my bicycle while returning home from my office at Western Seminary. I went around a corner, hit a patch of ice, my bicycle went out from underneath me, and I landed on my right hip. I knew instantly that I had done serious damage to my anatomy!

When I arrived at the hospital emergency room, what do you suppose I told the emergency room doctor? "Just give me a sedative so I can be at peace, and then let me go home." No way! I wanted the physician to deal with the problem, not just my pain! So I was taken into surgery and the broken hip was repaired with a long bolt, metal plate and four screws. It is the same way God deals with the damage we have all experienced because of sin. True peace cannot come apart from dealing with the fundamental cause of all our problems—our sin and separation from God.

The second major feature of the peace Christ promised is an *inward contentment*, the result of being at peace with God. This peace is the fruit of being rightly related to God through Jesus Christ (Gal. 5:22). This peace is not the kind of peace the world offers, for it is permanent and not based on favorable conditions or circumstances. Jesus promised "trouble" in the world (John 15:18-25; 16:1-4), but "peace" in Him (16:33). Paul referred to this peace as that "which surpasses all comprehension" (Phil. 4:7) for, unlike the peace that the world offers, Christ's peace—in inward contentment—is independent of external circumstances.

Haratio Gates Spafford (1828-1888) was a successful lawyer who lost most of his fortune in the great Chicago fire of 1871. The disaster was followed by an even greater loss. The Spafford family was scheduled to travel to Europe in November 1873. Being delayed by some last-minute business developments, Haratio sent his family on ahead. In the Atlantic Ocean their ship, the French liner *Ville duHavre*, collided with an English sailing vessel. Mrs. Spafford, who was rescued from the sea, cabled her husband the message, "Saved alone." Their four daughters had perished. In this supreme trial and test of his faith, Spafford penned the words of what has become a well-known hymn:

> When peace like a river attendeth my way,
> When sorrows like sea billows roll—
> Whatever my lot, Thou has taught me to say,
> It is well, it is well with my soul.

Such is the peace that Jesus offers—a peace based not on changing circumstances, but on an unchanging relationship with God through Christ.

Jesus reminds the disciples again of His impending departure by death and return at His resurrection. "You heard that I said to you, 'I go away, and I will come to you'" (John 14:28). Jesus then calls the disciples' attention to the way they responded to this revelation. "If you loved Me, you would have rejoiced, because I go to the Father." The disciples should have viewed Jesus' return to the Father as an occasion for rejoicing. But was it? Their thoughts were on themselves and what this loss would mean to them. They were apparently not loving Christ as they should. The love of which Jesus spoke was no mere emotion, but rather a sacrificial commitment to what was best for the other person. Jesus' return to the

Father was for His good and glory, but the disciples were focusing on themselves and found no joy in this announcement.

Jesus' words in verse 28, "For the Father is greater than I," are the basis of the theological error that regards Jesus as merely a created being and thus inferior to the Father. However, this statement must be understood in light of the clear words Jesus spoke in John 10:30, "I and the Father are One." Also in John 14:9 Jesus said, "He who has seen Me has seen the Father." Jesus clearly presented Himself as the divine Son of God, and John the Apostle wrote his Gospel to convince us of this truth (cf. 20:30-31). In what sense, then, is the Father "greater" than the Son? How can this be explained?

In relationship to Jesus' incarnation and His messianic office, the God the Father stands in a position of authority over Christ. While He is coequal with the Father in the Godhead, in his incarnation, Jesus became the submissive, obedient, subordinate Son for the accomplishment of His messianic mission (cf. 1 Cor. 11:3; Phil. 2:6-8). The concept of inequality is not suggested by any of these words. Jesus simply announced that He would return to the Father because it had been at the Father's command that He had come to earth to carry out His mission. Now Jesus wanted to report to His coequal, Commander-in-Chief that His mission had been fully accomplished (cf. John 17:4).

Jesus tells His disciples in 14:29 that He has announced His departure by death and return by resurrection prior to the events in order to elicit faith in His Word (cf. 13:19). When the disciples see that Jesus' words have been fulfilled and verified, they will trust in Him (cf. 20:28). Jesus then explains that His words will soon cease because of the present activity of Satan, "the ruler of the world" (cf. 12:31), soon to be carried out by Judas (14:30). While Satan has a claim on Judas (cf. 13:2,27), Jesus points out that "he has nothing in Me."

Referring to His impending departure by death, Jesus called His disciples' attention once again to the relationship between love and obedience. "But that the world may know that I love the Father, and as the Father gave Me commandment, even so I do" (14:31). Jesus is about to die in obedience to the commandment of the Father, and this will demonstrate to the world His love for the Father. Christ's death in obedience to the Father is intended to reveal His love (cf. 14:15).

John 14 concludes with the words, "Arise, let us go from here." The problem we encounter with this statement is that there are still three chapters remaining in the Upper Room Discourse and only in John 18:1 is Jesus said to have crossed the Kidron Valley on His way to the Garden of Gethsemane. Some have suggested that this phrase actually belongs at the end of the discourse and was mistakenly placed here by a later scribe. Others suggest that Jesus simply suggested that the disciples depart from the Upper Room at this point in the discourse, but they didn't actually leave until after chapter 17. But then the statement would be meaningless to the reader. Why would John have included it? I suggest that after Jesus said, "Arise, let us go from here," He and the disciples left the Upper Room for the Garden of Gethsemane. The rest of the discourse was probably delivered on the way to the garden and completed before they crossed the Kidron Valley (18:1). At any rate, we have to recognize that a major break in the discourse takes place at the end of chapter 14.

It is comforting to know that Jesus faithfully fulfills His Word. In fulfillment of His promise, the first century disciples of Jesus enjoyed the gift of the Holy Spirit, fellowship with the Triune God, and peace in the midst of a troubled world. The exciting news is that these promises are also meant for you and for me!

Study and Review Questions

1. Who is the "helper" Jesus promised the disciples? (John 14:16) How does the term "helper" describe His ministry?
2. Is the gift of the Holy Spirit only for believers? (14:17) Why is the unbelieving world unable to receive the promise of the Spirit? Is this gift of the Holy Spirit for all believers or only for extra spiritual believers? Cf. Romans 8:9, 14.
3. Describe the teaching ministry of the Holy Spirit (14:26). Was this ministry limited to the apostles?
4. Define the word "fellowship" in your own words. What kinds of Christian fellowship do you enjoy?
5. What would be the impact of Christ's resurrection on His disciples? Cf. 14:20,29.
6. Why did Judas (the other Judas, not Judas Iscariot) expect Jesus to disclose Himself to the world? (14:22). What prerequisites to this self-disclosure does Jesus require?

7. Describe the legacy of peace that Jesus promised His disciples (14:27). How is this different from the kind of "peace" the world offers?
8. What did Jesus mean when He said, "For the Father is greater than I"? (14:28). Does this suggest that the Son is an inferior being and less than God?

Chapter 7

A Disciple's Fruitfulness

John 15:1-11

Imagine for a moment that you are attending a funeral. As the soft, musical prelude concludes, the minister steps to the podium and begins the service.

"Dear family and friends, we are gathered here today to remember the life of one of our church members, Mr. *Professing* Christian. "Professing" joined our church thirty years ago when he prayed with our pastor and professed Christ as Savior. As you recall, his wife *Possessing* Christian, joined the church with him, and we have enjoyed many good years of fellowship with her. Unfortunately, Professing wasn't able to come to church very often. He sometimes worked on Sundays, and when he didn't have to work, his late Saturday night sessions at Joe's Pump House prevented him from attending our Sunday morning worship."

"When he professed Jesus as Savior, we had hoped to see Professing turn from the enticements of the world, devote more of his time to being a good husband and father, and evidence a desire to know more of the truth of God. But Professing Christian didn't have time for these things. When confronted with his lack of spiritual growth, Professing Christian would open his wallet to display a worn baptismal certificate. 'I am a Christian,' he would exclaim. 'Don't pressure me! I'll have more time for church when I retire.'"

"Last Friday night a massive heart attack suddenly ended Professing Christian's earthly life. We mourn his departure from us and covet his memory. But at least he was a Christian! At least he was saved! At least he is in heaven!"

I am sure that you too have known people who have professed Jesus as their personal Savior, but have never evidenced their genuine love for Him or demonstrated a desire to obey God's Word or manifested any fruit of the Spirit. But at least they prayed the prayer; at least they were baptized; therefore, they *must* be saved!

But I wonder if these outward activities really demonstrate that someone is a true follower of Jesus and guarantee that they are genuinely saved! Jesus helps us with this question in the next section of His Upper Room Discourse—John 15:1-11. Here we discover that the genuineness of a disciple's profession of faith is evidenced by fruitfulness in his or her personal life.

The Analogy of the Vine (15:1-2)

The disciples no doubt had walked through vineyards in Galilee and had observed the watchtowers where the farmers would stand guard over their crops as the grapes ripened. Certainly they were aware of the common metaphorical use of the vine in the Hebrew Bible where the nation of Israel was depicted as a vineyard (cf. Isa. 5:1-7; Psa. 80:14-15; Jer. 2:21; Ezek. 15:2-8). Jesus draws upon the familiar imagery of the vine and the branches to illustrate an important about what it means to have a personal relationship with God.

Fortunately, we are not left to our imaginations to decide what the vine represents in John 15, for Jesus Himself tells us. He said, "I am the true Vine, and My Father is the vinedresser" (15:1). The vine represents the Lord Jesus and the vinedresser (literally "farmer" or "cultivator") represents God the Father. The other element in the analogy given by Jesus is the "branches." In verse 5, Jesus told His disciples, "I am the Vine, you are the branches." Now while Jesus is addressing these words to His own disciples, it becomes apparent in the analogy that He is instructing them concerning *all* disciples—both the committed and those who only *appear* to be so.

We know from the Gospels that the word "disciples" can refer to Jesus' committed followers (cf. Matt. 10:1-3). But the word can also be used in a general sense of those who are curious or interested listeners with no firm commitment to Jesus. The multitudes to whom Jesus addressed His Sermon on the Mount were called "disciples" (Matt. 4:25-5:1; 7:28). Many of the hearers were unbelievers who wondered if the righteousness which they had by their Pharisaic practices and traditions was sufficient for their entrance into the kingdom of heaven (Matt. 5:20; 7:13,21). John 6:66 records that upon hearing Jesus' claim that He was "the Bread of Life," "Many of His disciples withdrew, and were not walking with Him anymore." Their commitment to Jesus was superficial, and they left Him when they were challenged to put their trust in His Person (6:60-64). As there were two kinds of disciples, so there are two kinds of branches—the fruit-bearing and the fruitless.

Jesus tells His disciples in John 15:2, "Every branch in Me that does not bear fruit, He takes away; and every branch that bears fruit, He prunes it, that it may bear more fruit." Let's first consider the fruit-bearing branches. They are pruned in order that they might bear more fruit.

The word translated "prunes" in verse 2 could be literally translated "cleanses," "purges," or "purifies." This is not the normal word for pruning, but Jesus used this word because he was talking about people, not just about vines.

Yamhill Country, west of Portland, has become a major wine producing district in recent years. In an article on Oregon vineyards, Robin Murto provides an insight on the importance of pruning. She comments, "Pruning is the single most important job you can do in a vineyard. What eventually ends up in a bottle of wine starts right here." Dick Shaw, whose 200-acre Yamhill County vineyard supplies grapes for some of Oregon's best winemakers, adds this comment, "Pruning isn't something that seems to intrigue people, but it is just absolutely critical. It's integral to the quality of the grapes. And if the quality isn't there, you are going to fail."

What is the point in Jesus' parable? As the vinedresser cuts away that which would hinder the productivity of the vine, so God the Father, through loving discipline, removes things from the lives of believers that do not contribute to their spiritual fruitfulness. The writer of Hebrews appears to have this "pruning" in mind when he points out that God disciplines His children. "For those whom the Lord loves, He disciplines, and He scourges ever son whom He receives" (Heb. 12:6). He goes on to say that while divine discipline seems to be joyful, but sorrowful, "afterward it yields the peaceful fruit of righteousness" (12:11). The "pruning" Jesus refers to in John 15 may not always be the result of sin, but rather designed to prevent it. The Apostle Paul was "pruned" by God. He had been greatly privileged to be caught up to paradise and experience unspeakable things. This unique opportunity gave Paul a tendency to boast, but God removed this tendency by giving him a "thorn in the flesh"—a physical affliction—to keep him from exalting himself (2 Cor. 12:1-7).

I experienced God's pruning early in my teaching career. I was still in my doctoral program when I was given the opportunity to teach a Bible class at Dallas Seminary. I was delighted with this assignment and worked hard to prepare and teach the class. At the end of the semester the dean provided the students with evaluations so they could critique my teaching. When I received back the evaluations, I was devastated by the critical comments. One student wrote, "Mr. Laney will never be a successful seminary teacher. He should go into the pastorate." It took me many months of reflection and prayer to recover from what I would identify as the most difficult time in my career. But as I look back on this experience I realize now that God was pruning me. He was cutting away a prideful attitude and the idea that I *myself* had something to offer students in the classroom. God was going to give me success in the seminary classroom, but He wanted me to learn early in my career that success and blessing would come from Him, not the result of my own intelligence, personal studies, or abilities. It was as if God immunized me against pride through that pruning experience. It is hard to be pruned! But God intends our pruning for good! He prunes us to make us more productive for kingdom ministry.

Now while the fruit-bearing branches are pruned to ensure greater fruitfulness, the fruitless branches "He takes away" (John 15:2). The words "takes away" mean "to lift up and carry away." The normal meaning of the Greek word used here (*airo*) is "to remove," not as some have suggested, "to lift up with a view to giving care." The latter interpretation would be excluded by verse 6 which describes the destruction of the fruitless branches. Who do the fruitless branches represent and what is their fate? Three main views have been set forth by Christian expositors.

One view is that the fruitless branches are true Christians who finally perish. They lose their salvation. This interpretation, however, is contrary to Christ's teaching in John 10:28, "And I give eternal life to them; and they shall never perish; and no one shall snatch them out of My hand." Those who have trusted Jesus and experienced the regenerating work of the Holy Spirit, are God's own children—forever.

Other evangelicals understand that the fruitless branches are true Christians who are removed to heaven by physical death as God's final step in discipline. While we know that God can discipline a believer with physical death (cf. 1 Cor. 11:30), the problem with this interpretation of God's dealing with the fruitless branches is that the removal described in verse 6 is a prelude to fiery judgment, not blessed fellowship with Jesus in heaven! While there are many texts that speak of a fiery destiny for unbelievers (cf. Matt. 3:12, 5:22, 18:8-9; 25:41; 2 Thess. 1:7-8; Rev. 20:15), there is no parallel in the New Testament where believers undergo a judgment by fire where they themselves are burned.

Still others take it that the fruitless branches are *professing* Christians who are ultimately severed from a superficial connection with Christ. According to this interpretation, fruitless branches represent those who make an external profession of faith which is not matched by a corresponding internal union with Christ. They may have prayed the prayer, professed faith, or been baptized, but they never genuinely trusted Christ and experienced the "new birth" which takes place through the ministry of the Holy Spirit (John 3:16; Titus 3:5). The fruitless branches are in fact *lifeless* branches! They are lifeless branches which are "thrown away," literally "cast out" (John 15:6). This is something that Jesus promised He would *never* do to a true believer. He said, "All that the

Father gives Me shall come to Me; and the one who comes to Me I will certainly not cast out" (6:37).

There is one problem with this view which sees the fruitless branches to be merely *professing* Christians. Some have argued that the presence of the phrase "in Me" (15:2) refutes the view that the fruitless branches represent unbelievers. However, the "in Me" may be understood in two possible ways. It can be interpreted as an adjective modifying "every branch." It can also be understood as an adverb modifying the words "bear fruit." It is quite significant that every other time "in Me" is used in John's Gospel, it is used *adverbally*. The sense of Jesus' words would be, "Every branch which does not bear fruit *in Me*, He takes away." The bearing of fruit depends upon "being" in Christ. The branch that does not bear fruit has no vital connection with the Vine. The fruitless branches are professing Christians who may have joined the church and been baptized, but somehow have never really trusted Christ personally. Like the uncommitted disciples who withdrew from Christ (cf. John 6:66), the fruitless branches are ultimately severed from their superficial connection with Christ. They may have attended church, taking communion and put money in the offering place. But none of these good things are the basis for our salvation. Only those with a genuine and life-giving connection with Christ the Vine will enjoy His presence forever.

The Prerequisite for Fruit-bearing (15:3-5)

In John 15:3-5, Jesus sets forth the essential key to fruitfulness in a disciple's life. He teaches that there is no fruit-bearing apart from an abiding relationship with Christ. Jesus spoke in verse 2 of the removal of the branch that bears no fruit. In verse 3, Jesus encouraged the disciples by revealing that He did not have them in view. He said, "You are already clean because of the word I have spoken to you." Jesus used the word "clean" earlier in the discourse in connection with the foot washing (13:10-11). The eleven disciples were "clean" by virtue of their response to Christ's Person and message, but Judas was "not clean" because he had committed himself to betraying Jesus. The message Jesus was telling His disciples in John 15:3 could be paraphrased, "Men, I know you are fruit-bearing branches because of your response to My message, but I'm giving you some instructions which will enable you to better understand why some branches bear fruit and others do not. I am giving this message to you, but its primary application will be to those to whom you minister—to those who claim to be My followers, but are not bearing fruit."

Jesus goes on to point out that abiding is absolutely essential for fruit-bearing. He said, "Abide in Me, and I in you. As the branch cannot bear fruit of itself, unless it abides in the vine, so neither can you, unless you abide in Me. I am the Vine, you are the branches; he who abides in Me, and I in him, he bears much fruit; for apart from Me you can do nothing" (15:4-5). The Greek word "to abide" (*meno*) literally means "to stay" or "to remain." It is used of someone (or something) who remains where he is. Realizing that some of the ship's crew planned to escape from the doomed vessel, Paul said to the centurion and the soldiers, "Unless these men remain (*meno*) in the ship, you yourselves cannot be saved" (Acts 27:31). The word is also used figuratively of someone who does not leave the realm or sphere in which he finds himself. Jesus said to the Jews who had believed in Him, "If you abide (*meno*) in my words, then you are truly disciples of Mine" (John 8:31). Where the word is used figuratively in John's writings, "abiding" is virtually the equivalent to "believing" in Jesus.

In His Bread of Life Discourse, Jesus says, "For this is the will of My Father, that everyone who beholds the Son, and believes in Him, may have eternal life; and I Myself will raise him up on the last day" (6:40). Later, confronting the Jews with the necessity of their assimilating His person, Jesus says, "He who eats My flesh and drinks My blood has eternal life; and I will raise him up on the last day" (6:54). Then in verse 56 He links the "eating and drinking" with "abiding." Jesus said, "He who eats My flesh and drinks My blood abides in Me, and I in him." Here is how I visualize the relationship between these concepts:

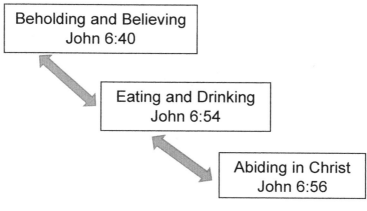

Also in 1 John, the author equates confessing Jesus with abiding (4:15). In 1 John 3:24, he equates obedience (the mark of genuine faith, cf. John 3:36) with abiding in Christ. The gift of the Holy Spirit is set forth by John as a sure evidence of such an abiding relationship with Christ (1 John 3:24; cf. Rom. 8:9, 14). The one who allows the Gospel message to abide in his heart "will abide in the Son and in the Father" (1 John 2:24).

What we are discovering from these verses is that believing in Jesus establishes a relationship of abiding in Christ. Belief is the connection which unites the Vine and the fruit-bearing branches. Apart from this vital connection with Christ the Vine, there can be no abiding and hence no fruit-bearing! Jesus points out that He abides in the one who abides in Him. This relationship of mutual abiding results in the production of "much fruit." As the absence of fruit on the branch indicates that it is not abiding in the vine, so the absence of fruit in the life of a professing Christian indicates that he or she is *not* abiding in Christ. What kind of branch would not bear fruit? A *dead branch*, of course! Fruitlessness, then, is the mark of "deadwood." A fruitless "Christian" may be one who has made a profession of faith but has no vital relationships with Christ the Vine.

John illustrates what may be called "superficial belief" in several places in his Gospel. Some people in Jerusalem were believing in Jesus because of His miracles, but Christ apparently judges this "belief" as superficial and was not trusting them (John 2:23-25). Many of the multitude "believed in Him," but they were not sure that Jesus was the Messiah (7:31). Jesus challenged those Jews who had "believed" Him to demonstrate the genuineness of their faith by abiding in His Word (8:31). Later He pointed out that they wanted to kill Him and did not believe His word (cf. 8:40, 45-47). There are, then, those who manifest a superficial attachment to Christ but do not commit themselves to the point of saving faith. The problem seems to be with the *content* of their faith. They believed in His miraculous signs or something about His powerful preaching, but did not trust Jesus as their personal Savior.

The Destiny of the Fruitless Branches (15:6)

What happens to the fruitless branches which Christ "takes away"? (15:2). Jesus describes their future destiny: "If any one does not abide in Me, he is thrown away as a branch, and dried up; and they gather them, and cast them into the fire, and they are burned" (15:6). Don't confuse this burning with that described by Paul in relationship to the Judgment Sea of Christ. Paul says that every believer's works will be tested by fire, and only those which pass the test will be rewarded (1 Cor. 3:12-25; 2 Cor. 5:10). At the Judgment Seat of Christ, works are burned, but at the judgment described in John 15, *people* are burned. While ever believer will undergo the Judgment Seat of Christ for reward or loss of reward, no believer will undergo a judgment in which they themselves are burned. Such a destiny awaits unbelievers only (cf. Rev. 20:15).

The fruitless branches in John 15 represent professing Christians who have no vital connection with Christ the Vine. According to verse 6, they are "cast into the fire and they are burned." This refers to the biblical doctrine of eternal punishment. Satan, the master Deceiver, wants to prevent people from enjoying the presence of Jesus eternally and deceives them into following him to hell.

I believe that Satan sometimes allows people to get just enough of "Christianity" to immunize them against the real thing. Children are given an immunization shot against diphtheria, whooping cough and tetanus. Through the injection, they are given just enough of these bugs to cause their immune system to build up antibodies against a full-fledged encounter with these diseases.

Satan operates on the same principle. He doesn't seem to mind if people join a church, get baptized, or put money into the offering plate. If not properly instructed, well-meaning people go through these rituals thinking such activities are a means of salvation. After they have had their religious experience, they are, as it were, "immunized" against authentic Christianity.

Ask them, "Are you saved?" They respond, "Of course! I tithe and am a member in good standing at my church." If that is their answer, it is likely that Satan has them just where he wants them—deceived into thinking they are going to heaven when in fact, they have no life-giving relationship with Christ the Vine.

The Results of Abiding in Christ (15:7-11)

If abiding in Christ results in fruit-bearing, what fruits would you expect the fruitful branches—the true disciples—to produce? It is clear from Scripture that Jesus expects Christians to reproduce themselves (Matt. 28:19-20), but this does not appear to be the fruit Jesus had in mind here. Was Jesus suggesting that true believers will produce the "fruit of the Spirit"? (Gal. 5:22-23) Perhaps, but I believe that the "fruit" Jesus had in mind for the disciples to produce is indicated in the context of John 15. In verses 7-11, five specific fruits are mentioned.

The *first* result or fruit produced by an abiding relationship with Christ is answered prayer. Jesus said, "If you abide in Me, and My words abide in you, ask whatever you wish, and it shall be done for you" (15:7). The Father will answer the prayers of those who have a life-giving connection with Christ the Vine because of the Person and work of His Son (cf. 14:13-14). Note the breadth of the promise, "Ask whatever you wish, and it shall be done for you." This does not mean that if Christ has not answered your prayers, you are not a true disciple. The answer may be forthcoming, or perhaps the request is not according to God's will (cf. 1 John 5:14-15) and the answer is no. But as praying Christians, we need to have the expectancy expressed by the country preacher who began a prayer meeting with the words, "Brothers and sisters, here you are coming to pray for rain. I'd like to ask you just one question—where are your umbrellas?"

The *second* fruit of abiding in Christ is that the Father is glorified. "By this is My Father glorified, that you bear much fruit, and so prove to be My disciples" (John 15:8). God is glorified through the life of a branch which is in a vital relationship with Jesus the Vine. What does it mean "to glorify God"? It simply means to magnify or exalt the estimation in which God is held by others. God is glorified through the lives of believers who cause others to have a higher view of His person and work. Has your life caused others to have a higher estimate of the character of God? Have you exalted His reputation? If so, you are bearing fruit!

The *third* fruit produced by a branch which is abiding in Jesus is a love relationship with Jesus. "Just as the Father has loved Me, I have also loved you; abide in My love" (15:9). Jesus reveals to His disciples that His love for them is like the Father's love for Him. The one who abides in Christ's love will have a love for others (cf. 1 John 4:7-21) and be motivated by his or her sacrificial commitment to obey Christ's commands (John 14:15).

The *fourth* fruit of abiding in Christ is revealed in 15:10. "If you keep My commandments, you will abide in My love; just as I have kept My Father's commandments, and abide in His love." Abiding in Christ means to love Jesus, and to love Him means to obey Him (14:15). Closely associated with this fruit of obedience would be a desire to know God's Word. Jesus said, "If you abide in My Word, then you are truly disciples of Mine" (8:31). How can you obey the teachings of Jesus if you don't read and study God's Word?

The *fifth* fruit produced in the life of a disciple abiding in Christ is joy. Jesus concluded His exposition of the analogy of the vine and branches with these words, "These things I have spoken to you...that your joy may be made full" (15:11). Unlike happiness, the joy believers have is not based on "happenings." Rather, Christian joy is deeply rooted and grounded in a personal relationship with Christ. The branch which abides in Christ has Christ's own joy—a joy that is full and overflowing.

Some people have asked, "How much fruit ought a fruit-bearing branch produce?" Jesus seems to answer that with his words, "He bears much fruit" (John 15:5). I would say on the basis of John 15:1-11 that there will be at least *some* fruit in the life of every genuine believer.

The amount or quality of the fruit may vary depending on the maturity and spiritual state of the Christian. The amount of fruit produced by a grape vine varies depending on the pruning, fertilizing, and watering it receives. But a living branch connected to a vine will produce *some* fruit. Similarly, there will always be some fruit in the life of a genuine believer. The five fruits mentioned in John 15:7-11 appear to be basic and suggestive. They probably do not exhaust the kinds of fruit a Spirit filled disciple can produce. The ones mentioned in the immediate context may amount to the minimal or basic fruits which would provide evidence of an abiding relationship with Jesus.

Are You a Fruitless or a Fruit-bearing Branch?

The message Jesus set forth for His disciples in John 15:1-11 is simply that *fruitfulness results from abiding with Christ.* If there is a genuine connection with Christ the Vine, then there will be some fruit—a productive prayer life, a life that glorifies God, a love for Christ and others, a desire to learn and obey Christ's Word, and a joy that is independent of circumstances.

The absence of fruit is an evidence of unbelief. John 15:1-11 reveals that a branch without fruit has no vital connection with Christ the Vine. Just like Mr. Professing Christian, there may be some who have become involved in Christianity without ever becoming *true* followers of Jesus. Their fruitless lives are the evidence that demonstrates their lack of genuine saving faith. It is not that they lost their salvation. Rather, they were never saved in the first place.

Now you may be asking, "Is this truth unique to John's Gospel, or is it revealed elsewhere in Scripture?" I have found the truth of John 15:1-11 confirmed throughout the New Testament. John the Baptizer exhorted the Pharisees and Sadducees who were coming for baptism to "bring forth fruit in keeping with your repentance" (Matt. 3:8). Jesus told the multitudes listening to His Sermon on the Mount, "You will know them by their fruits.... Every tree that does not bear good fruit is cut down, and thrown into the fire" (7:16, 19). James wrote, "Faith, if it has no works, is dead, being by itself" (James 2:17). Commenting about the Cretans, Paul declared, "They profess to know

God, but by their deeds they deny him, being detestable and disobedient, and worthless for any good deed." (Titus 1:16). John wrote in his first epistle, "The one who does not love does not know God, for God is love" (4:8). A few verses later he drove the point home with the words, "If someone says, 'I love God,' and hates his brother, he is a liar" (4:20). Throughout God's Word we find the truth that fruitfulness results from having a life-giving relationship with the Lord Jesus Christ.

I am afraid that there are a lot of people in our churches today who are in the same spiritual condition as Mr. Professing Christian. They may claim to be Christians, but by the test of fruitfulness we would have to conclude that they are lifeless branches destined for burning.

I don't want genuine followers of Jesus to doubt their salvation after reading this chapter. But I do want them to *be sure* they are saved. Paul told the Corinthians, "Test yourselves to see if you are in the faith; examine yourselves!" (2 Cor. 13:5a).

Remember the lesson from John 15:1-11, fruit-bearing authenticates a person as a true follower of Jesus while fruitlessness indicates the sobering reality that a person has no vital connection with Christ the Vine.

You can make sure you have that connection simply by *trusting* in Jesus' atoning work on the cross and receiving Him as your personal Savior today.

Study and Review Questions

1. Identify the elements in the analogy found in John 15:1-2. Can you explain what each of the elements represents?
2. How does the Father deal with the fruit-bearing branches? What are some of the processes God uses to cause believers to bear more fruit?
3. What do the fruitless branches represent? How should the phrase "in Me" (15:2) be understood?
4. What does it mean to "abide" in Christ? (15:4-5). Does this compare with any other New Testament term? Why is abiding in Christ a prerequisite for fruit-bearing?
5. Explain the fate of the fruitless branches. How can we be sure that the fruitless branch is not a Christian (cf. 6:37)?
6. How might a fruitless branch be found within the fellowship of a local church? What steps could we take to prevent people from thinking they are genuine Christians when in fact they are not?
7. What are the results of abiding in Christ? What specific fruits should Jesus' disciples look for in their lives?
8. Is the teaching in John 15:1-11 unique to John's Gospel? Where else do we find the principle that "fruit-bearing results from abiding in Christ"?

Chapter 8

A Disciple's Friend

John 15:12-17

Only a few weeks after we had moved to Dallas, Texas to study at Dallas Theological Seminary, Nancy and I began to realize what it meant to be a friend. Nancy had just begun a new job at Southern Methodist University working as a secretary for the football coaches. It turned out to be a great job because she always got free tickets to the SMU Mustang's football games! One bright morning about 7:45 I discovered that the battery in our car was dead. Now, had this happened in Portland where I had spent the last four years, I would have had many friends I could call at a moment's notice to help me start the car. But we had just moved to Dallas and didn't know anyone we could call for help.

I began to panic. Nancy had to be at work in a few minutes. What would I do? As I tried to figure out a solution, a young man stepped out of the apartment across the courtyard from ours. He was a total stranger, but I was desperate. I called out and told him my situation. He was on his way to classes at Baylor Dental School, but was kind enough to help me with my car. Using jumper cables, we soon had my car running.

As Nancy drove off to work that morning (she even got there on time!), I determined that I would develop some new friends in Dallas. I had experienced, for a brief moment that morning, what it was like to be without a friend in a time of need. I didn't want to be in that situation again.

As Nancy and I spent the next three years living in Dallas, some very fine friendships developed. These friendships made our years at Dallas Seminary some of the best of our lives. After we returned to Oregon to teach at Western Seminary, we continued a relationship with our friends in Dallas and cultivated new friendships Portland.

I am sure that you have special friends too. These friendships are truly a gift from God. As Solomon said long ago, "There is a friend who sticks closer than a brother" (Prov. 18:24). What then, does it mean to be a friend? And what does it mean to be a friend of God?

In this chapter we will discover who is the disciple's *best* friend and identify the keys to developing that relationship.

The Basis of Friendship (15:12)

John 15 focuses on the subject of "relationships"—the relationship of Christ and His disciples (15:1-11), the relationship of the disciples with one another (15:12-17), the relationship of the disciples with the world (15:18-25), and finally, the relationship of the disciples with the Holy Spirit (15:26-27). While the relationship of Jesus with His disciples is one of "abiding," the relationship of the disciples with each other is to be one characterized by "love." This is the clear teaching of Jesus in John 15:12. "This is My commandment, that you love one another, just as I have loved you." Here Jesus repeats the thrust of the new commandment, emphasizing the believer's responsibility to love one another (John 13:34-35).

The new commandment serves as the basis for a believer's relationships with other disciples. Two brief reminders concerning the new commandment may be helpful. *First,* the kind of love spoken of by Jesus in John 13:34-35 and 15:12 is identified by the Greek word *agape.* This love is not an emotion or a feeling that can come or go depending on the circumstances of the moment. *Agape* love is a sacrificial commitment to the ultimate good of another person. It is a volitional love, a love that is the result of a personal decision rather than a circumstantial or temporary emotion. *Second*, this agape love for one another is a commandment, not merely a suggestion. Believers have a responsibility, based on the new commandment, to exercise sacrificial commitment in dealing with one another. The command of Jesus to love one another is the basis or foundation for rich and growing friendship among disciples.

It is very special when God brings close friends into our lives with whom we have a natural affinity based on common interests, backgrounds, and ambitions. I have a good friend who has served as pastor in a number of different churches in Oregon. We attended seminary together and have common interests in teaching, preaching, and *fishing!* For many years we have enjoyed

131

an early spring fishing trip together. When we are together, the conversation flows nonstop as we discuss theology, moral and political issues, books we have read, and *future* fishing trips. We have watched each other's children grow up and become parents themselves. We have prayed for each other through painful and difficult situations which we have both faced. I have really appreciated this special, lifelong friendship. But I have had other relationships that took more effort to cultivate.

During my college days at the University of Oregon, I worked on summer staff as a chef's helper at a Christian conference center. Working in the kitchen at that time was a woman whom most of the summer staff quickly grew to dislike. She was crabby and bossy, and most of my friends in the kitchen tried to avoid her. I decided that I would take her on as a "summer project" and try to win her friendship. I would do my best to be thoughtful and kind through my words and actions. I made a diligent effort to go out of my way to be courteous, avoid conflict and to listen to her complaints without striking back. As the summer went on, she began to trust me and share with me a little about her background and life experience. Her husband had left her, and she was very bitter about it. She felt that the world was down on her. Life had been tough on her, and she compensated by being tough on others.

By the end of the summer, I had a much better understanding of this woman and felt a genuine affection for her. She had responded to my *agape* love, and a genuine friendship had developed. Reflecting on this relationship I recall that I first had to demonstrate love to this woman by faith in obedience to Christ's commands. It was only later that the warm feelings of friendship began to develop in this relationship. I believe this is the way God planned for Christian relationships to develop. Are you in need of friend? Then be a friend! Decide to love someone sacrificially and watch that relationship begin to blossom!

The Pattern of Friendship (15:13)

The sacrificial aspect of the believers' love for one another is highlighted by Jesus in verse 13. "Greater love has no one than this, that one lay down his life for his friends." Most of us would willingly sacrifice our lives to save our children, or even to save a spouse. But would we die for a friend? Truly, that would be the ultimate expression of sacrificial love.

David Lucas, an eighteen-year-old college student, and his uncle, Bill Quinlan, left San Diego on a sailing trip to the Galapagos Islands, 600 miles west of Ecuador. Their forty-foot trimaran was a sturdy vessel which could ride out an ordinary tropical storm, but the hurricane they unexpectedly encountered on the tenth day of their trip wasn't an ordinary storm. When the vessel capsized, they abandoned the boat for an inflated rescue raft and managed to survive the treacherous storm. But the only provisions in the raft were five ten-ounce cans of water and two small packages of rations.

Since the men were not expected to arrive in the Galapagos for several weeks, they knew it would be a long time before they were missed. They both knew that the meager provisions they had on the raft would not sustain them long in the hot tropical sun. After four days of drifting in the sea, Bill reflected on their situation. "If we're going to survive we have to do it ourselves," he said.

"But what can we do?" David asked.

"You can't do anything," Bill replied. "But I can get in the water and just swim out of sight." Bill pointed to the remaining cans of water at their feet. "If you try, you could stretch these for five or six days. You could last three or four days after that."

David was horrified at this suggestion. But as the next day dawned, Bill gave David his wedding ring, scratched a farewell to his wife and children on an empty water can, slipped into the water, and swam away. He didn't turn back. Several days later, after David had consumed the last can of water, the crew of a tuna boat spotted the nearly collapsed life raft. After his recovery from severe dehydration, David told the story of his uncle's sacrifice at sea.

Jesus said, "Greater love has no one than this, that one lay down his life for his friends." Jesus Himself is such a friend. Paul writes, "For one will hardly die for a righteous man; though perhaps for the good man someone would dare even to die. But God demonstrates His own love toward us, in that while we were yet sinners,

Christ died for us" (Rom. 5:7-8). It is a rare thing for a man to die for a friend. But Jesus goes beyond such an expression of sacrifice in giving His life for His enemies—even for those who crucified Him! What an amazing example of friendship! What a powerful pattern of friendship for believers to emulate!

The Characteristics of Friendship (15:14-15)

In John 15:14-15, the relationship between Christ and His disciples is defined as a "friendship." The believers are called Christ's "friends." Jesus said, "You are My friends, if you do what I command you. No longer do I call you slaves; for the slave does not know what his master is doing; but I have called you friends, for all things I have heard from My Father I have made known to you."

The New Testament uses the term "friend" (*philos*) two ways. Luke 15:29 illustrates the *normal* use of the term. The self-righteous son declared to his father, "For so many years I have been serving you, and I have never neglected a command of yours; and yet you have never given me a kid, that I might be merry with my *friends*." But there is another use of the term that provides great insight into what Jesus is saying about His relationship with His disciples. The *technical* use of the term "friend" is reflected in John 19:12 where the Jews declared to Pontius Pilate that if he released Jesus he would show himself to be no "friend of Caesar."

To be called "a friend of Caesar" (corresponding to the Latin *amici Caesaris*) in the first century was to receive the highest title and honor anyone could enjoy in relationship with the Roman government. It meant precisely four things: *First*, you knew the emperor intimately. "Friends of Caesar" would open the emperor's mail and carry out his correspondence. *Second*, you were willing to go wherever the emperor sent you. The "friends of Caesar" were often sent to the provinces to carry on the emperor's business. They would represent Rome's interests in the provinces and conduct Caesar's affairs. *Third*, a friend of Caesar would retain the title and position even if the emperor died, for a friend of Caesar was always a friend of Rome. *Fourth*, a friend of Caesar would avoid the loss of this privileged relationship at all cost, for if you failed in your duties or betrayed the emperor it meant your political doom.

The historical background of the term "friend," as it was used in a technical way in the time of Jesus, enables us to better understand His words when Jesus calls His disciples "friends." Jesus reveals that their status as His "friends" is conditioned on their obedience (15:14) and results from their intimate knowledge of Him (15:15).

So what characterizes a disciple who is a "friend of Jesus." First, to be Christ's friend means to obey Him willingly. Some Christians are experts at finding excuses for not obeying Jesus and His teachings. "That doesn't apply to us because it's in the Old Testament," or "that's based on first century culture," they say. Jesus taught that our obedience to His Word is the measure of our love for Him.

Garcia Iniguez was a Cuban patriot and outstanding military leader who suffered wounds, imprisonment, and deprivation of family life during his 30-year struggle for Cuban independence from Spain (1868-98). Once while Garcia was hiding out in the jungles of Cuba, the Cuban rebel leaders not yet in hiding urgently needed to contact him. But they didn't know where he was or how to reach him. Three commandos were selected as candidates to take the message to Garcia. They were individually briefed on the situation, warned concerning the difficulties and dangers involved, and then asked the question, "Are you ready to take the message to Garcia?" The first commando responded, "I would need time to plan and prepare for this mission." He was dismissed from the assignment. The second said that he would be willing if he had six men to assist him. He was thanked for his willingness but also dismissed. Finally, the third commando was briefed. He was told of the urgency of the mission and the dangers involved. Then he was asked the question, "Are you ready to take the message to Garcia?"

He paused, breathed deeply, and reported, "I am ready." This is the kind of dedicated obedience and commitment that truly delights the heart of God. This is the attitude of those who are Christ's friends.

Second, to be Christ's friend means to know Him intimately. A slave knows *about* his master but does not know him *personally* (cf. 15:15). I know about the President of the United States, but I do not have a personal relationship with him. To be a friend of Christ means that you don't just know about Him, but you have a vital, growing, personal relationship with Him. Consider the story of Mary and Martha (Luke 10:38-42). Martha was busy attending to the preparations for the meal while Mary fellowshipped as a disciple at the feet of Jesus. Martha's service was necessary, but its significance was temporary. Jesus said that Mary had chosen the "good part"—the development of her relationship with Christ. This would have lasting meaning and significance. Many of the disciples I know are like Martha. They are busily involved in the church program—teaching Sunday School, serving as a deacon, or being a youth group leader—but have little time for Jesus Himself. We are running a fantastic three-ring circus while Jesus is sitting of to the side saying, "I appreciate your efforts to advance My kingdom, but come and spend some time with Me. Getting to know Me personally takes priority over all the things you are doing for Me."

The Responsibilities of Friendship (15:16-17)

Responsibilities are the inherent by-product of friendships. We all feel an obligation to help our friends when they move, need a ride to the airport, or when they have car trouble. During my years of teaching at Western Seminary, Nancy and I have made lots of friends. And when these friends face challenging or unexpected circumstances, we like to respond and help. It may just be an encouraging card, a loaf of fresh baked bread or a meal delivered to their home, but we know that being a true friend requires a positive response to our friends when they have a need. So too, our friendship with Christ means that we have some responsibilities as His friends. In John 15:16, Jesus reveals that His disciples are obligated to a mission and a ministry. He said, "You did not choose Me, but I chose you, and appointed you, that you should go and bear fruit, and that your fruit should remain, and whatever you ask of the Father in My name, He may give to you."

Jesus points out in the first part of verse 16 that our friendship with Him is by His choice, not ours. It was His initiation that we obtained our reconciliation with God. How encouraging to know that Jesus reached out to us and invited us to be His friends! He also appointed His disciples for a *mission* ("go") and a *ministry* ("bear fruit"). The fruit mentioned here probably refers to service leading to the conversion of lost sinners. Why else would the disciples be commanded to "go"? In connection with this ministry, they are again promised that their prayers in Jesus' name will be effectual (cf. 14:13-14). Jesus concludes this section of His discourse as He began it, with a restatement of the new commandment (15:12). A believer's relationship with Christian brothers and sisters should be marked by sacrificial (*agape*) love.

Who, then, can be regarded as a friend of Jesus? A friend of Jesus is one who knows Him intimately and obeys Him willingly. Abraham is called a "friend of God" (James 2:23; Isa. 41:8; 2 Chron. 20:7). He knew God intimately and obeyed God willingly. Abraham obeyed God's command to take his son to the land of Moriah and sacrifice him as a burnt offering on a mountain there

(Gen. 22:1-3). And his intimate knowledge of God's person and power gave him confidence that the God who could bring life to Sarah's barren womb could resurrect Isaac out of the tomb (cf. Gen. 22:5; Heb. 11:17-19). A friend of God is characterized by uncompromising obedience to Christ's commands and intimate knowledge of His person and work.

Does Jesus regard you as a friend? Do you know Him intimately and obey Him willingly? If not, this would be a great day to begin your personal relationship with Jesus by trusting Him and His wrath-absorbing sacrifice for your sins. Jesus actually *died* for you. And He wants to be your *best* friend!

Study and Review Questions

1. Describe the "love" Jesus commands His disciples to have for one another (John 15:12). Can you show agape love without feeling personal affection?
2. How did Jesus model *agape* love for His disciples? (15:13; cf. 10:11; 13:1; Eph. 5:1-2,25; Gal. 2:20). List several ways you can exercise sacrificial love for your spouse or your best friend.
3. What is the historical background of the term "friend" as used by Jesus in John 15:14-15? Where in John's Gospel is the term also used in this technical sense?
4. What does it mean to be a "friend" of Jesus? Evaluate your own friendship with Christ on a scale of

one to ten. What area in your own life is most in need of your attention to be *more* of a friend of Jesus?

5. What are several practical steps you can take to develop your personal relationship with Jesus and get to know Him better?

6. Our friendship with Jesus has obligations. What obligations or responsibilities are mentioned by Jesus in John 15:16-17?

7. Why do you suppose the new commandment is reiterated again in John 15:17 (cf. 13:34-35; 15:12)? Does this suggest something concerning its importance to Jesus?

Chapter 9

A Disciple's Hostile World

John 15:18-25; 16:1-4

Stan and Pat Dale were missionaries to the Yalis, a tribe of cannibals who ruled the eastern mountain highlands of Irian Jaya, Indonesia. The Yalis called themselves "Lords of the Earth," for in their remote mountain valleys no one challenged their dominion. In league with the evil spirits they worshiped and served, the Yali warriors bowed to no one! Little did Stan know when he began his work of the complexity of his mission to bring the good news of the gospel to the Yalis, or how chilling the hazards were which awaited him. Seven years later, on September 25, 1968, Stan Dale and his missionary colleague, Phil Masters, were martyred under a hail of Yali arrows.

Stan and Phil were exploring some isolated mountain valleys in search of new airstrip sites. In his book, *Lords of the Earth* (Regal Books, pp. 304-05), Don Richardson tells the story of Stan and Phil being confronted by a band of hostile Yali warriors.

> A warrior-priest named Bereway slipped around behind Stan and—at point blank range—shot an arrow in under his upraised right arm. Another priest, Bunu, shot a bamboo-bladed shaft into Stan's back, just below his right shoulder.

…As the arrows entered his flesh, Stan pulled them out, one by one, broke them and cast them away. Dozens of them were coming at him from all directions. He kept pulling them out, breaking them and dropping them at his feet until he could not keep ahead of them. Soon, some thirty arrows had found their mark in Stan's body….

Stan faced his enemies, steady and unwavering, except for the jolt of each new strike. Yemu, a new Yali believer, ran to where Phil stood alone. Together they watched in anguish at Stan's agony. As some fifty or more warriors detached from the main force came toward them, Phil pushed Yemu behind him and gestured speechlessly—*run!* Phil seemed hardly to notice the warriors encircling him. He eyes were fixed on Stan.

Fifty arrows—sixty! Red ribbons of blood trailed from the many wounds, but still Stan stood his ground. The attack had begun with hilarity, but now the warriors shot their arrows with desperation bordering on panic….

"Fall!" they screamed at Stan. "Die!" It was almost a plea—*please* die!

Yemu did not hear Phil say anything to the warriors as they aimed their arrows at him. Phil made no attempt to flee or struggle. He had faced danger many times but never certain death. But Stan had shown him how to face it, if he needed an example. That example could hardly have been followed with greater courage.

Once again, it was Berway who shot the first arrow. And it took almost as many arrows to down Phil as it had Stan.

Jesus told His disciples on the night before His own death, "If they persecute Me, they will also persecute you.... An hour is coming for everyone who kills you to think that he is offering service to God" (John 15:20; 16:2). While we might tend to think that these words apply only to the apostles of old, the martyrdom of Stan Dale and Phil Masters illustrates just how relevant is Jesus' teaching about a disciple's relationship with the unbelieving world.

In his book, *The Global War on Christians* (Crown Publishing, 2013), John Allen writes, "Christians today indisputably are the most persecuted religious body on the planet." According to The International Society for Human Rights, 80% of violations of religious freedom in the world today are directed against Christians. There is a consensus that 2015 was one of the worst years in history for persecution against Christians. Kurt Nelson, president and CEO of East-West Ministries, concurs. He states, "Jesus was pretty clear on indicating that things were going to go from bad to worse. I think we are seeing that played out in the twenty-first century. Persecution of Christians is clearly on the rise."

John 15 deals with relationships. The relationship between Jesus and His disciples is characterized by *abiding* (15:1-11). The relationship between believers and one another is to be characterized by *agape*--sacrificial love (15:12-17). But the relationship between the followers of Jesus and the unbelieving world will be marked by hatred and hostility. In this chapter we will examine the *reason* for the world's hatred of Jesus' disciples, the *extent* of this hostility, and *how* 21st century disciples can handle it.

The Reasons for the World's Hostility (15:18-21)

Having repeated once again the new commandment to "love one another" (15:17), Jesus reveals by way of contrast that the world's attitude toward His disciples will be one of hatred and hostility. "If the world hates you, you know that it has hated Me before it hated you" (15:18). The Greek grammar of verse 18 indicates that the world's hatred is actual, not hypothetical as the English translation might suggest. The verse could be translated, "*Since* the world hates you,…" The "world" Jesus refers to here is the unbelieving world of mankind, particularly those who are part of Satan's world system which is intensely hostile toward God (cf. John 12:31; 15:19; 17:14). The world *will* have such an attitude of hostility toward believers, but Jesus reminds the disciples that this is nothing new. The words, "You know," are probably a command. In other words, Jesus is saying, "Since you are going to experience the world's hostility, be comforted in knowing that nothing new has befallen you. The unbelieving world hated Me first!"

Jesus goes on in verses 19-21 to explain to the disciples three *reasons* for the world's hatred toward His followers. The first reason is the essential difference in nature between the world and Christ's disciples. "If you were of the world, the world would love its own; but because you are not of the world, but I chose you out of the world, therefore the world hates you" (15:19). The world loves its own—those who belong to its system, commend its values, and follow its ways. The word "loves" refers to a personal affection (*phileo*) rather than the sacrificial commitment (*agapeo*) referred to in verse 17. While the world has an affection for its own kind, it hates those who have been delivered out of the darkness into the light of Christ. The unbelieving world hates those faithful believers, regardless of color, ethnic background or age, who have turned their backs on wickedness to pursue a life of righteousness as followers of Jesus.

The second reason given by Jesus for the world's hostility against believers is their identification with the rejected Christ. Jesus said, "Remember the word that I said to you, 'A slave is not greater than his master.' If they persecuted Me, they will also persecute you; if they kept My word, they will keep yours also" (15:20). Since the world persecuted Jesus, the unbelieving world will naturally extend that persecution to His followers.

To elucidate this truth, Jesus draws an illustration from the servant-master relationship which was so well known in the first-century culture. A servant would never be greater than his master in privilege or protection. As in verse 19, the Greek grammar indicates that the word "if" could be translated "since" in both places where it appears in verse 20. Since Christ was persecuted, then His disciple-servants can expect to be persecuted as well. On the other hand, since some obeyed Christ's words, turning to Him for salvation (cf. Jn. 3:36), they would also obey the disciples' message. The disciples could expect to fellowship with Jesus in His suffering and to share as well in His success.

The third reason given by Jesus for the world's hatred of the believers is their ignorance of the Father. Jesus told His disciples, "But all these things they will do to you for My name's sake, because they do not know the One who sent Me" (15:21). The inevitable hatred and persecution of Jesus' disciples by the unbelieving world springs from the fact that the world does not know God! Rejection of the Son is the same as rejection of the Father (cf. 15:23), and it logically follows that those who reject both will reject Jesus' disciples (15:21). Could I expect to be welcomed with open arms by Kim Jung Un, the Supreme Leader of North Korea? Probably not. The dictator would certainly associate me with freedom loving America and no doubt be suspicious of my friendly overtures. So it is with those who have a hatred for God the Father. They express similar hostility for His Son and those who faithfully serve Him.

When was the last time you experienced the hatred or hostility of the unbelieving world for being a follower of Jesus? If you are rubbing shoulders with unbelievers through your work, ministry, or living situation, you very likely have experienced the ill will if not the open hostility of unbelievers toward you. This ill will may manifest itself in your being passed by for a job promotion, criticized for your stand on moral issues, or ignored by some people in the lunchroom at your work place. When I participated in a televised forum considering the issue of whether or not scientific creationism should be taught in our public schools as a viable alternative to the evolutionary hypothesis, I felt rather keenly the hostility of those with an opposing view. My viewpoint was termed "unscientific, religious dogma" and its advocates regarded as ignorant fools. Jesus promised that His disciples would face such hostility. He warned, "I chose you out of the world, therefore the world will hate and persecute you, just as it has Me."

Prediction of the World's Hostility (15:22-25)

Jesus goes on in vv. 22-25 to explain that the world's hatred of Jesus and His followers is inexcusable, yet inevitable, for it comes in fulfillment of biblical prophecy. Jesus appeals to His *words* and *works* to demonstrate that the world has no excuse for rejecting Him. His appeal to His words is reflected in verse 22: "If I had not come and spoken to them, they would not have sin, but now they have no excuse for their sin." Had Jesus not come and testified of His relationship with the Father, the Jews of the first century might be excused for rejecting Him. They would still be sinners in need of a Savior, but would not be guilty of the specific sin of rejecting Christ's words. Yet since Jesus *had* come and spoken to the unbelieving world, offering Himself as Lord and Savior, the world stood guilty for rejecting Him.

Christ's second appeal is to His works. He said, "If I had not done among them the works which no one else did, they would not have sin; but now they have both seen and hated Me and My Father as well" (15:24). Had Jesus *not* performed His authenticating miracles, those who rejected Him might have had some excuse. But again, this was not the case. His public miracles pointed to the truth of His person (cf. 20:30-31), but this testimony was rejected. Consequently, those who rejected Him were without excuse and stood condemned for refusing the evidence of His powerful words and miraculous works. In rejecting Jesus, they rejected the Father as well (15:23-24) and were left in their state of sin and condemnation.

Verse 25 reveals that the world's hatred was inevitable because it was prophesied in the Hebrew Bible. Jesus said, "But they have done this in order that the word may be fulfilled that is written in their Law, "They hated Me without a cause'" (15:25). Psalm 35:19 and 69:4, which are quoted by Jesus, speak of a hatred which lacks any reasonable foundation. This is precisely the kind of hatred that the unbelievers in the first century demonstrated toward Jesus, the divine Messiah.

As objectionable as it is, the world's hatred of God's Son was according to prophecy. Peter, in his sermon on the Day of Pentecost, said that Jesus was delivered up to death at the hands of godless men and by the predetermined plan of God (Acts 2:23). It is important to remember, however, that while God was sovereign over Christ's rejection, evil people were responsible for their actions. The sovereignty of God never cancels out human responsibility.

People are responsible and accountable before God for what they say and do. God is not the author of evil (cf. James 1:13,17). But He is sovereign over evil and can even use it to accomplish His purposes (cf. Ps. 76:10). This truth is reflected in the words of Joseph to his brothers who sold him into slavery. He said, "And as for you, you meant evil against me, but God meant it for good in order to bring about this present result, to preserve many people alive" (Gen. 50:20). If God can use the evil actions of evil people to accomplish His purposes, think of what He can do through the good works of His fully committed disciples!

The Extent of the World's Hostility (John 16:1-4)

After a brief word concerning the believers' relationship with the Holy Spirit (15:26-27—we will save this text for the next chapter), Jesus continues to develop the concept of the world's hatred of believers. In 16:1-4, Jesus informs His disciples that this hatred will result in severe persecution. Jesus has not just been rambling in this great discourse. His message is purposive. He has forewarned His disciples of their coming trials so that they "may be kept from stumbling" (16:1). The word "stumble" is a metaphor that pictures one falling over an unexpected obstacle. Jesus is telling His disciples, "Since the path ahead is dark, I'm warning you beforehand of the obstacles in your path so you won't be taken by surprise and overcome by your trials."

Jesus goes on to reveal to the disciples the extent of the trials they will face. "They will make you outcasts from the synagogue; but an hour is coming for everyone who kills you to think that he is offering service to God" (16:2). Like the blind man who turned to Jesus after being healed, the disciples could expect to be excommunicated from the synagogue (9:34)—cut off from all normal dealings with the Jewish community. This was considered a drastic measure in the first century A.D. since it meant that the excommunicated Jew would forfeit all social relations and religious privileges connected with the synagogue and temple worship. A time will come, warns Jesus, when men's values will be so perverted that the one who kills you will think that he is serving God! The word "service" (v. 2) speaks of *religious* service or worship. This prediction was realized in the life of Saul of Tarsus who persecuted the early Christians out of a sincere desire to serve God (cf. Acts 26:9-11; Phil. 3:6; 1 Tim. 1:13).

Apparently sensing the need to again explain to the disciples the reason for this extremely severe persecution, Jesus says, "And these things they will do, because they have not known the Father, or Me" (John 16:3). The persecutors of the disciples are ignorant of the Father and Son (cf. 15:21). While they may know *about* God, their persecution of the disciples would indicate that they do not know Him *personally* as revealed through His Son.

Finally, in verse 4, Jesus gives the reason for His warning at this particular time. "But these things I have spoken to you that when their hour comes, you may remember that I told you of them. And these things I did not say to you at the beginning, because I was with you" (16:4). With His departure imminent, it was necessary for the disciples to be informed of these matters so when persecution came they would remember Jesus' words and be encouraged by them. An account in the Book of Acts indicates that the words of Jesus served their purpose. When the apostles disobeyed the Sanhedrin's order to stop preaching about Jesus, they were flogged and commanded once again to speak no more in Jesus' name. Luke tells that when they departed from the presence of the Jewish Sanhedrin, the disciples were "rejoicing that they had been considered worthy to suffer shame for His name. And every day, in the temple and from house to house, they kept right on teaching and preaching Jesus as the Christ" (Acts 5:42-42).

The Experience of the World's Hostility

As we conclude our study of this section of the Upper Room Discourse, I invite you to consider three questions. My first question: Did the world's hatred and hostility which Jesus warned His disciples about manifest itself during their lives and ministry? It certainly did! The Book of Acts records the flogging of the apostles (Acts 5:40), the martyrdom of Stephen (7:54-60), the persecution against the Jerusalem church (8:1-2). James was executed (12:2), Peter was imprisoned (12:3-4), and Paul was stoned at Lystra (14:19). Later Paul and Silas were imprisoned at Philippi (16:19-25). The list of hostilities against Jesus' followers could go on and on!

According to church tradition, the Apostle Andrew was crucified. Bartholomew was clubbed, flayed alive, and then crucified. Thomas was pierced with a lance while kneeling in prayer. Peter was crucified head down at Rome, and Paul was beheaded during the reign of Nero. Yes, the words of Jesus were literally fulfilled in the experience of the apostles. All the apostles suffered for Christ sake, and many gave their lives for their Christian witness.

My second question: Are Christ's disciples being persecuted today? Again, I must answer with a resounding yes! One of my colleagues at Western Seminary who spent several years teaching school in a Moslem country tells of a young college student who trusted Jesus as his Savior. His father was so angered by the young man's conversion that he hired three men to kill his own son! When Ceil Rosen, the wife of Moshe Rosen (founder of Jews for Jesus), trusted Christ, her parents literally disowned her. They said, "We'll just forget that you're our daughter and that will be the end of that." Her parents move to Israel, and she was never able to contact them again.

Chester Bitterman, working with Wycliffe Bible Translators' Summer Institute of Linguistics, was taken captive by Marxist guerrillas in Colombia. His captors threatened to execute him if his fellow translators and linguists did not leave Colombia. The Wycliffe translation team refused to give up their work of translating the Scriptures and stayed in Colombia. Forty-eight days after the kidnapping, Chet's bullet-riddled body was found in an abandoned bus in Bogota, Colombia. More recently, twenty-one Coptic Christians were lined up on a beach in Libya with their hands bound behind their backs. Behind each was a masked Islamic State soldier dressed in black and wielding a knife. As the Christians sang quietly and prayed, they were forced down and beheaded. One of my students, a pastor serving in East Africa, reported how a suicide bomber drove his car into his church setting off an explosion that killed many worshipers. Another African student sent a prayer letter telling of the beheading of an evangelist by Muslim extremists. These are just a few of the example of the world's hatred and hostility being perpetrated against Jesus' followers in the twenty-first century. Yes, Christ's disciples are being persecuted today. And such persecution is on the rise.

My third question: How are we as Christians going to handle the world's hostility when we experience it? I believe that there are three keys to coping with persecution—however mild or intense. First, recognize the *reality* of the persecution of believers. The work of God never goes on without being met by the world's opposition. We are in a spiritual battle and we have an enemy (Satan) who is seeking to destroy us. Don't be taken by surprise or caught off guard when persecution comes your way. Second, realize the *reason* for the persecution. Persecution takes place because of your identification with the rejected Christ. The hostility you experience is nothing personal. It is not so much a hatred against you but against the One you represent. Third, respond to persecution with love and prayer for the persecutors. Jesus said, "Love your enemies and pray for those who persecute you" (Matt. 5:44). Jesus gave us an example to follow. Shedding His blood for those who rejected Him, Jesus prayed on the cross, "Father, forgive them; for they do not know what they are doing" (Luke 23:34). And if death should come as a result of persecution, Stephen shows us how to face martyrdom. Luke records, "Then falling on his knees, he cried out with a loud voice, 'Lord, do not hold this sin against them!' Having said this, he fell asleep."

Study and Review Questions

1. What characterizes a believer's relationship with the unbelieving world in contrast to his relationship with other Christians?
2. Is the world's hatred hypothetical or actual? (John 15:18) How have you experienced the hostility of the unbelieving world?
3. What three reasons does Jesus give for the world's hatred toward His followers? (15:19-21)
4. Why does all the world stand guilty and without excuse for their rejection of Jesus (15:22-24).
5. What is the quotation from Psalm 35:19 and 69:4 designed to demonstrate in John 15:25?
6. How do you relate the sovereignty of God in the rejection of Jesus with the accountability of those who rejected Him?
7. To what extent would the world's hatred be experienced by Jesus' first century disciples? (16:2) Did the world's hostility become a reality for them?
8. How can followers of Jesus cope with living in a hostile world? I have suggested several ideas. Can you think of others?

Chapter 10

A Disciple's Helper

John 15:26-27; 16:5-15

My first date with the college girl who became my wife was at the Fox Hollow Roller Rink on the south side of Eugene, Oregon where we both attended the University of Oregon. I remember well that special evening and the "couples only" skate where I took Nancy's hand in mine for the first time and we skated to the sound of romantic music.

Little did I realize as I drove her home from the roller rink, this evening was the beginning of what would develop into friendship, love, marriage and a life together. Roller skating is good, wholesome fun. I can definitely recommend a roller skating date!

When I was a little kid, we had metal, clip on roller skates that came with a "key" to adjust the skates and fasten them to your own shoes. But at the roller rink, we rented shoe skates which were especially made for roller rinks. Now the skating technology has advanced to roller blades! I am sure you have seen people zipping along the streets and sidewalks on roller blades with helmets, padded knees and elbows, and maybe talking on their cell phones.

I remember when my son, John, received his first pair of roller skates. Although he was only five, he quickly became an excellent skater. He could skate frontwards, backwards, and even in circles—as long as I was *holding his hand!* When I let go of his hand, he would easily loose his balance and take a tumble. Fortunately, at five-years old, he was still pretty close to the ground and no injuries result from his first attempts to "solo" on his Spiderman skates.

As a little boy, John enjoyed skating. But he enjoyed it most when his little hand was tightly held in mine, giving him the security, confidence, and protection that any beginner skater needs.

Life is a lot like skating. It offers difficult challenges, the joy of accomplishment, and many opportunities for bumps and bruises. Fortunately for Jesus' disciples, we have a Helper who has taken our hand and committed Himself to staying with us, not just through the beginning lessons, but throughout life. That Helper is the Holy Spirit.

In this chapter, we will focus on the ministry of the Holy Spirit. We will first consider His ministry to the unbelieving world. Then we'll discover how the Holy Spirit comes alongside Jesus' disciples to provided assistance and stability as they skate along through life.

Witnessing for Christ (15:26-27)

Although Christ's disciples have been called to be witnesses to a hateful, hostile world (cf. 15:18-25), there is a word of encouragement in John 15:26-27. They don't face that hostile world alone! The Holy Spirit has been appointed to bear witness with the disciples concerning the Person and work of Christ. Verse 26 reveals three things about the Holy Spirit—His titles, origin, and work. The Holy Spirit is first referred to as "the Helper." This title suggests that He is One who comes along to assist, empower, and encourage a believer. As I gave fatherly assistance to my son while he was learning to roller skate, so the Holy Spirit provides divine assistance as He personally indwells every genuinely born again believer (cf. Rom. 8:9,14; 1 Cor. 12:13). The designation "Spirit of Truth," also used of the Holy Spirit in verse 26, suggests that He is characterized by and communicates truth. This aspect of His person is essential to His ministry of teaching the disciples, as we will see in John 16:12-15.

Verse 26 revels the origin of the Holy Spirit. Jesus refers to Him as the One "whom I will send to you from the Father." Since John 14:26 revealed that the Father would send the Spirit in Christ's name, we must conclude that the sending of the Spirit is an activity that concerns them both. The statement that the Holy Spirit "proceeds from the Father" was the basis for the decision of the Synod of Toledo (A.D. 589) to add the clause "and the Son" to the words of the Constantinople Creed (A.D. 381) regarding the "procession" of the Spirit. While much has been made of the *Filioque* (Latin for "and the Son") clause, the main thrust of verse 26 concerns the mission of the Spirit. The mission of the Holy Spirit is to bear witness to the Person and work of Jesus (see John 16:5-11).

Chapter 15 concludes with the words, "And you will bear witness also, because you have been with Me from the beginning" (15:27). The primary ministry of *both* the Holy Spirit and the disciples in relationship to the unbelieving world is that of *witness*—testifying concerning the person and work of Jesus. The disciples would be able to carry out this ministry because of what they had seen and heard as they fellowshipped with Jesus from the beginning of His public ministry. What an encouragement to know that Jesus' disciples always have a partner when they share their faith. They are co-witnesses with the Holy Spirit! When we share our faith with our next-door neighbor, a child at Sunday School, or a clerk at the grocery store, the Holy Spirit is with us, always impressing on the hearts of unbelieving people the truth of Jesus Christ.

On May 6, 1970 I faced the most challenging witnessing opportunity of my college career. For several months, I had been working with Christian groups at the University of Oregon to organize a rally at the Free Speech Platform to be followed by a "March for Christ" around the U. of O. campus. Our purpose was to present Jesus as the answer to the spiritual needs of the Oregon collegians. Although our rally wasn't scheduled until 11:30 A.M., when I arrived on campus about 9 A.M., I found that hundreds of students were already gathered on the lawn in front of the Free Speech Platform. Before the platform were four simple crosses which had been hastily erected as a memorial to the students killed by the National Guard at Kent State University just the *day before*. The students were tense and the atmosphere was explosive. There was talk of a student strike. How providential that we had planned our rally for this day!

Since the Free Speech Platform could not be reserved, we were in danger of having a radical campus group take the platform and not relinquish it for our rally at

11:30. After consulting with several student leaders, we decided to mobilize the Christians and start the rally early. We took the Free Speech Platform and witnessed to a throng of students from 9:30 to 11:30 when our main speaker, a black pastor, Rev. Wendall Wallace, arrived. We took turns speaking from the platform about our personal experiences with the Savior, Jesus. While one student spoke, others prayed or shared Christ with students milling around the platform.

As our rally concluded, over 1,000 followers of Jesus joined in a "March for Christ" around the U. of O. campus. Many students carried signs reading, "God is alive and well in Oregon," "Jesus frees us," "Jesus loves radicals too!" I rode in a sound truck sharing the Gospel as we moved along. The Lord used our efforts in a significant way to confront many students with the claims of Jesus Christ. It was an exciting experience!

Looking back, I realize that the key to our successful witness on that memorable day is found in John 15:27. The Holy Spirit was present at the Free Speech Platform. He was with us as we marched. He was witnessing to the hearts of U. of O. students concerning Jesus as many student disciples spoke a word for their Lord that day. The Holy Spirit is always present with believers, co-witnessing concerning the person and work of Jesus.

Convicting the World (16:5-11)

In John 16:5-11, Jesus elaborates on the witnessing ministry of the Holy Spirit and shows how He accomplishes it. Jesus referred to His departure to the

Father earlier in the discourse (13:33; 14:3), but now He speaks as if He is "on His way" home. "But now I am going to Him who sent Me" (16:5a). Jesus' words, "And none of you asks Me, 'Where are You going?'" (16:5b), present a problem. Peter had asked about Jesus' departure in John 13:36. Jesus' words probably reflect the fact that their questioning was not persistent. The disciples' thoughts were on their own immediate loss, not on how the prospect of leaving affected Jesus.

Jesus' announcement of His departure brought gloom to the disciples' faces and filled their hearts with sorrow (16:6). For the disciples, Jesus' departure seemed disastrous, but in reality it was for their benefit. In verse 7, Jesus gives the disciples a word of encouragement by pointing to the positive benefit that would result from His departure. "But I tell you the truth, it is to your advantage that I go away; for if I do not go way, the Helper shall not come to you; but if I go, I will send Him to you" (16:7). Without the departure of Jesus, there would be no coming of the Spirit.

Now, in what way is the indwelling presence of the Holy Spirit more desirable than Christ's personal presence among His disciples? *First*, while Jesus could not always be with the disciples (cf. John 6:17), the Holy Spirit is universally present in every believer (Rom. 8:9). *Second*, while Jesus was on earth, the disciples were sometimes fearful (cf. John 6:20; Mark 14:50). But after the coming of the Spirit, they spoke for Christ with a new confidence and boldness (Acts 4:31). *Third*, while Christ's stay on earth with the disciples was temporary, the Holy Spirit's stay would be permanent (John 14:16). In light of Jesus' departure to heaven, God the Father provided His disciples with One who would be their friend and helper forever—the Holy Spirit!

In John 16:8-11, Jesus expands on 15:26, explaining the means by which the Holy Spirit will witness to the unbelieving world. The Holy Spirit will bear witness to the person and work of Christ by doing the work of *conviction*. "And He, when He comes, will convict the world concerning sin, righteousness, and judgment. The word "convict" is a legal term meaning to cross examine for the purpose of convincing or refuting an opponent. It implies a rebuke which brings conviction. The word used here means awakening or proving guilt. The Holy Spirit will act as a prosecuting attorney to bring about the world's conviction before God in relationship to three things—sin, righteousness, and judgment.

The Holy Spirit will first convict an unbeliever regarding "sin." What sin in particular is Jesus referring to? He explains, "Concerning sin, because they do not believe in Me" (16:0). The Holy Spirit secures a verdict of guilty against the world because of the sin of *unbelief*. The greatest demonstration of sin against God is unbelief—the rejection of His own precious Son. We don't need to fuss with our non-Christian friends over their excessive drinking, marijuana smoking, illicit sex or other sinful activities. There is only one sin that prevents them from being saved—the sin of unbelief! (cf. 3:18). As you witness to unbelieving friends, focus on the importance of trusting Jesus as personal Lord and Savior. The Holy Spirit, working through the Word of God, will take care of the needed changes in lifestyle. Besides, without the

163

indwelling ministry of the Spirit, it is pretty much impossible to change one's behavior or live a holy life.

The second ministry of the Holy Spirit to unbelievers is to convict them "concerning righteousness." Jesus adds the explanatory phrase, "Because I go to the Father, and you no longer behold Me" (16:10). In Acts 3:14, Peter refers to Jesus as the "Holy and Righteous One." Christ's return to the Father is the ultimate proof that He is the perfect pattern of righteousness that God accepts. The Holy Spirit will work to convict unbelievers of their failure to accept the standard of righteousness which God approves—that righteousness exemplified in the Person of Jesus Christ.

Finally, the Holy Spirit convicts the world "concerning judgment." Jesus explains, "Because the ruler of this world has been judged" (John 16:11). Since Satan, the ruler of the world stands judged because of the cross (cf. 12:31), what chance is there for a mere human to escape judgment if God's grace is refused? *No* chance! Those who follow Satan will share His ultimate destiny (cf. Matt. 25:41; Rev. 20:7-15).

There is a logical order to the convicting ministry of the Holy Spirit in relationship to an unbeliever. *First* of all, the unbeliever needs to see his state of sin from God's perspective. *Then,* he needs to know that only the righteousness of Jesus can save him. *Finally*, he must be reminded that if he refuses Christ's provision, he faces certain judgment and condemnation. Where do you stand in relationship to the convicting work of the Holy Spirit? Have you responded to His witness and trusted Jesus for your salvation?

It was an Easter Sunday when I first remember experiencing the convicting work of the Holy Spirit. I realized during the pastor's message that I was a sinner and needed a Savior. When the pastor gave an invitation to receive God's gift of salvation, I knew that I should do that. I later spoke to my mother about my desire to be saved. She directed me to the pastor of our church, Dr. Vance Webster, and he explained what Jesus had done to pay the penalty for my sins and how I could place my trust in Him as my personal Savior. At the age of ten, I professed my faith in Jesus and was immersed (or *baptized*). The Holy Spirit had carried out His initial ministry in my life. But as we will see in the next section, His work was far from being over.

Teaching the Disciples (16:12-15)

In John 14:26, Jesus had told the disciples that the Holy Spirit "will teach you all things, and bring to your remembrance all that I said to you." The Holy Spirit is the ultimate Teacher of Jesus' disciples (cf. 1 John 2:27). As I encourage my first-year seminary students to maintain a teachable spirit throughout their training, I jokingly tell them that if they claim Psalm 119:99a as their life verse, "I have more insight than all my teachers," then when they take their final exam they might have to confess with David in Psalm 35:11b, "They ask me things that I do not know." Well, we all have lots to learn. My seven years of formal theological education have made me all the more aware of just how much I have yet to learn in the vast field of biblical studies. Professor Howard Hendricks, master teacher at Dallas Seminary, once said, "The key to being a good teacher is to be a good student—a learner among learners." I wholeheartedly agree!

In John 16:12-25, Jesus elaborates on the teaching ministry of the Holy Spirit. He begins by informing the disciples that He has more to tell them, but at present they would be unable to cope with this information. "I have many more things to say to you, but you cannot bear them now" (16:12). Why were the disciples unable to bear further teaching from Jesus at this time? *First*, the disciples were limited in their ability to perceive the truth because they did not have the Holy Spirit to illuminate it for them. *Second*, they were presently unable to live out the implications of the revelation. Only when they received the Holy Spirit would they have the power to make practical application of this truth. What then is the Holy Spirit's ministry to Jesus' disciples?

First, the Holy Spirit will guide believers into all truth. Jesus said, "But when He, the Spirit of truth, comes, He will guide you into all the truth; for He will not speak on His own initiative, but whatever He hears, He will speak" (16:13a). The word "guide" is made up of two words in the original Greek--"to lead," and "the way." It suggests that the Holy Spirit will "lead the way" to the truth.

Notice that Jesus says "all the truth." The Holy Spirit "gives it to us straight." There is no error, compromise, or variation in the truth He communicates. This is because the Holy Spirit speaks exactly what He hears from Jesus, and Jesus speaks what He hears from the Father (7:16). The Spirit, like the Son, will not lead the disciples into a "truth" that is distinctive from that which the Father would reveal. There is infinite consistency and harmony in the revelation of the Triune God. By way of application, the Holy Spirit guided the apostles in what to write as divine revelation. Now since God's revelation has been completed in Christ (cf. Heb. 1:2), the Holy Spirit's ministry to Jesus' disciples today is that of making clear the meaning of the inspired record. This is the ministry of *illumination* (cf. 1 John 2:27).

A second ministry of the Holy Spirit to believers is revealed in John 16:13b, "And He will disclose to you what is to come." The word "disclose" means to "report" or "announce." The phrase "things to come" refers to prophetic events. In other words, *after the departure of Jesus, the Holy Spirit would report or announce prophetic events to the disciples.* This promise was directed to apostles like Peter and John to whom prophetic events-- *things to come*--would be revealed. For disciples today, it is as they study the Scripture that the Holy Spirit helps them understand God's prophetic program.

The study of biblical prophecy is of great benefit, but also has some subtle dangers. I believe that the greatest danger is the tendency to focus on the *messenger* rather than the key *message* of prophecy. The Apostle John failed in this area. He fell at the feet of the angelic messenger, but was rebuked with the words, "Do not do that; I am a fellow servant of yours and your brethren who hold the testimony of Jesus; worship God. For the testimony of Jesus is the spirit of prophecy" (Rev. 19:10). In other words, the study of prophecy should witness to the person and work of Christ—the coming King! Make sure that Jesus is kept on center stage in any study of biblical prophecy.

A third ministry of the Holy Spirit to believers is to disclose the things of Christ. Speaking of the Holy Spirit's ministry, Jesus said, "He shall glorify Me; for He shall take of Mine, and shall disclose it to you. All things that the Father has are Mine; therefore, I said, that He takes of Mine, and will disclose it to you" (John 16:14-15). The Holy Spirit will *glorify* Christ as He declares the truth of His person. It is significant that the Holy Spirit works to glorify Jesus rather than to draw attention to Himself. This truth gives us an insight into determining what works are genuinely of the Holy Spirit. Jesus will be glorified as the Holy Spirit takes truth which Jesus has received from the Father and communicates it to His disciples. The Holy Spirit, our indwelling Helper, not only witnesses with us concerning the Person of Christ, but also leads us into the way of all God's truth. What a unique and special Friend we have!

As a disciple of Jesus, have you lost your bearings spiritually? Are you uncertain as to your direction in life or what is true regarding some biblical doctrine teaching? The world can be enemy territory for followers of Jesus as they try to make their way around spiritual minefields, hindrances to a growing faith, and questionable teachings.

Disciples of Jesus need someone to come alongside and show the safe path. Allow the Holy Spirit to be *your* guide. Jesus promised that the Holy Spirit would be our teacher, and lead us into *all* truth.

Study and Review Question

1. What ministry does the Holy Spirit share with the disciples in relationship to the unbelieving world? (15:26-27)

2. In what way is the indwelling presence of the Holy Spirit more desirable than Jesus' personal presence among His disciples? (16:7)

3. The Holy Spirit will bear witness to the Person of Christ by doing a work of conviction. What is the meaning of the word "convict"? (16:8). What was this like in your own life?

4. Do you see a logical order in the Holy Spirit's ministry to unbelievers? Explain how this is significant.

5. Why were the disciples unable to bear further teaching from Jesus at the time He addressed them in the Upper Room? (16:12)

6. How does the Holy Spirit minister to Jesus' disciples? (16:13-15)

7. Did the Holy Spirit minister to the apostles as authors of Scripture in a somewhat different manner than He ministers to 21st century believers?

8. To whom does the Holy Spirit attract attention? How can this truth be helpful and instructive to disciples today?

Chapter 11

A Disciple's Victory

John 16:15-33

It was a hot, humid day in Dallas, Texas, but the perspiration on my brow was more the result of nervous tension than the weather. It was the day of my oral comprehensive exam for my doctoral program at Dallas Seminary. My dissertation, "Selective Geographical Problems in the Life of Christ," had been completed and approved. But now I faced the toughest test of all. I was responsible for the content of the whole Bible and was instructed to be prepared to defend my doctoral dissertation.

Would I be able to recall what I had studied, or would I experience a brain freeze and forget even my own name under the intense questioning? As the hour for the exam approached, my stomach began to tighten. I tried to appropriate Jesus' promise of peace (John 14:27), but the anxiety would not leave me completely. So much depended upon passing this exam. I had already been invited to a faculty position at Western Seminary. Would they rescind the invitation if I failed my comprehensive exam?

Just after I entered the dean's office, Dr. Dwight Pentecost, my major professor, walked in. He could see that I was more than a little nervous, so he gave me some words of encouragement that got me through the day. Dr. "P" said, "Carl you have done well in your program, and I am confident that you will do just fine today."

Sensing Dr. Pentecost's confidence in me, I became more calm and confident as I approached the exam. The questions were challenging and there were some awkward moments as my brain searched its' data bank for answers. But I walked out of the dean's office two hours later having made the final hurdle on my way to graduation. I had passed my oral comprehensive exam!

What an encouragement Dr. Pentecost's words were to me just before I waded into the deep waters of the dean's office! I am confident that Jesus' words to His disciples just before His departure and death would have been of similar encouragement. At the end of Jesus' Upper Room Discourse, Jesus spoke some words of encouragement to His faithful disciples. He spoke to them about their future joy (16:16-24), their personal faith (16:25-30), and their ultimate victory (16:31-33).

A Believer's Perfect Joy (16:16-24)

The disciples were about to experience the deep sorrow of seeing their Master, Jesus, executed on a Roman cross. For them, this would be a time of great sorrow and remorse. Jesus announced that in a very short time He would pass from their sight, but shortly thereafter the disciples would see Him again. "A little while, and you will no longer behold Me; and again a little while, and you will see Me" (16:16). The disciples were quite perplexed by this announcement and asked each other, "What is this thing He is telling us?" (16:17) The source of their difficulty was the phrase, "a little while." They confessed their own lack of comprehension of Jesus' words (16:18). They simply had no idea what Jesus was talking about.

As the disciple had difficulty with Jesus' words in verse 16, so have the commentators. At least three views have to be considered. Some expositors understand Jesus to be saying that the disciples' spiritual insight ("will see") will be followed by His own physical departure ("no longer behold"). However, there is no clear distinction between the verbs "to see" (*horao*) and "to behold" (*theoreo*). They appear to be used as synonyms in verse 16. Others take it that Jesus is saying that His Second Coming will be followed by His ascension to heaven. But then we must stretch the "little while" to over 2,000 years! A third suggestion is that the "little while" refers to the three days between Christ's death and resurrection. This view coincides nicely with Jesus' words in John 14:18-19. The point is that Jesus' resurrection appearances would follow shortly after His death. Jesus would die, but three days later ("a little while") He would appear to His disciples in His resurrection body.

The cryptic reference to His death is followed by a further explanation to the still perplexed disciples. "Truly, truly, I say to you, that you will weep and lament, but the world will rejoice; you will be sorrowful, but your sorrow will be turned to joy" (16:20). The disciples would weep at Christ's death while the unbelieving world rejoiced. But the sorrow of the disciples would be turned to joy! The disciples' sorrow over the crucifixion would be surpassed by their rejoicing over His *resurrection*!

Jesus likens the disciples' sorrow over His death to the travail which a mother endures giving birth. "Whenever a woman is in travail she has sorrow, because her hour has come; but when she gives birth to the child, she remembers the anguish no more, for the joy that a child has been born into the world." (16:21). Childbirth is first a cause of pain, but when the child is born, the distress is all but forgotten!

I never really appreciated the truth expressed in this illustration until the birth of our first child. It was around 2 A.M. when Nancy woke me up and said, "This is it! Our baby is on the way!" Still groggy from deep sleep I thought, "Can't this wait until morning?" But when a baby is coming, there is no way to delay the process! Once I was alert and dressed, we began to put into practice the breathing exercises we learned in our childbirth classes. The exercises are designed to keep the mother concentrating on something other than the pain of the contractions. Later, at the hospital as the contractions became more frequent, the breathing kept us busy—but there was still plenty of pain as the labor intensified. However, when that pink little boy had safely arrived and was cuddled in Nancy's arms, the sorrow of labor gave way to rejoicing for God's gift of a son. To be quite honest, Nancy still remembers the pain of her first delivery, but the joy we have experienced through the life of our son has far surpassed the pain of delivery. (Yes, I know, that's easy for *me* to say.)

The great London preacher, Charles Haddon Spurgeon (1834-92), once said, "There is a sweet joy that comes to us through sorrow." This truth is expressed quite clearly by Jesus, "Therefore you, too, now have sorrow; but I will see you again, and your heart will rejoice, and no one takes your joy away from you" (16:22). The disciples would have sorrow over Christ's departure—but Jesus would return to them in His resurrection body. And then they would have joy! Notice that in contrast to their *temporary* sorrow over His death, their joy over His resurrection would be *permanent*!

How is it that Jesus could promise His disciples permanent joy? Would they always be happy? After the resurrection, would the disciples never have a "bad day"? It is helpful, I believe, to distinguish *joy* from *happiness*. A simple illustration will help you see the difference. In the vicinity of my home in Portland, Oregon, there are two rivers—the Columbia and the Willamette. Whether it is summer or winter, rainy or dry, these rivers always have water in them. There may be some fluctuation depending on the season, but never in the known history of Oregon have these river channels ever been dry. On the other hand, in the city of Dallas, Texas, where I attended seminary, there is a different kind of river.

One hot August day as I drove across a bridge over the Trinity River, I was amazed to see nothing but green grass and mud in the Trinity River channel. Later that fall, after some rain, I happened to drive across the Trinity River again. This time the banks of the river were about to *overflow* from all the muddy water! Now the difference between the Trinity and the rivers in Portland is that the Trinity River fills after a rainstorm, but the Columbia and Willamette have a *constant* source of water from the melting snow in the Cascade mountains. This is how it is with happiness and joy. Happiness is the result of *happenings*, whereas joy is the result of a *relationship with Jesus*!

We all have within us a channel that is capable of being filled with happiness as the channel of the Trinity River can be filled with water. But the happiness based on circumstances is short-lived. Jay Gould, an American financier and multimillionaire, said when dying, "I suppose I am the most miserable man on earth." Someone said that money won't make you happy, but it will make misery much more bearable. I believe Mr. Gould would disagree. Alexander the Great conquered the known world of his day and then wept, "There are no more worlds to conquer." Voltaire, the French philosopher of world renown, wrote, "I wish I had never been born."

The words of these men demonstrate that happiness continues as long as the circumstances are favorable, but like the Trinity River, there are times when it "runs dry." But for those who have a relationship with Jesus, there is a *constant* source of joy. They may run low on happiness because of life's circumstances, but disciples of Jesus need never run out of joy!

As believers, we can have joy—a deep sense of gladness and gratitude to God—even in the midst of difficult circumstances. Joy is not based on changing circumstances, but on an unchanging relationship with Jesus. It is the fruit of being rightly related to God through Christ. Paul includes "joy" in his list of the fruit of the Spirit (Gal. 5:22). Unlike happiness, the joy we received from Jesus cannot be snuffed out or taken away (John 16:22).

Jesus goes on to instruct the disciples that in the day of His resurrection and thereafter, they will have no need to question Him further about His teaching. When they receive the illuminating ministry of the Holy Spirit, there will be no need for questions such as "Where are You going?" "How do You know the way?" "What is this that He says, 'A little while'?" (cf. 13:36; 14:5; 16:18) Their questioning of Jesus would be replaced with prayer to the Father.

Jesus reveals three keys which will enable His disciples to experience full joy. The *first* key is found in John 16:24, "Until now you have asked for nothing in My name; ask, and you will receive, that your joy may be made full." Full joy is the portion of those who pray to the Father in Jesus' name—on the basis of His merits and influence (cf. 14:13-14). God the Father will answer such prayers in order that Jesus' disciples may experience *full* joy! It is significant that the joy Jesus promised His disciples is dependent and conditioned on prayer. Believers are to pray *in order that* our joy may be made complete. Perhaps when we are without joy, it is because we have failed to pray.

A *second* key to experiencing joy is to hear and heed Jesus' commands (cf. 15:10-11; 17:13). There is no joy for those who live in total disregard of God's Word. To disobey the instruction of Jesus in God's Word is to experience only guilt, avoidable problems and deep regret. A *third* key to experiencing a constant flow of joy is to maintain fellowship with Jesus and other Christians (cf. 1 John 1:3-4). When we distance ourselves from Jesus and God's people, we are lonely, isolated and joyless. On the other hand, when we are praying, obeying, and in fellowship with Christ and His followers, we are essentially "walking in the Spirit" (Gal. 5:16) and the fruit of joy will be full and abundant in our lives (5:22).

The Disciples' Profession of Faith (16:25-30)

Jesus encourages the faith of His perplexed and apprehensive disciples by promising them more clear teaching after His resurrection. He begins, "These things I have spoken to you in figurative language; an hour is coming, when I will speak no more to you in figurative language, but will tell you plainly of the Father" (16:25). Up to this time in His ministry, Jesus had spoken enigmatically—through parables, allegories, and figures with interpretations which were not always apparent. But the use of such enigmatic statements would soon cease. During His forty-day post-resurrection ministry (Acts 1:3), Jesus would declare the truth of the Father to spiritually enlightened men. Instruction through parables and figures would then be unnecessary.

Jesus goes on to promise His disciples direct access to the Father based on the merits of His name. "In that day you will ask in My name; and I do not say to you that I will request the Father on your behalf; for the Father Himself loves you, because you have loved Me, and have believed that I came forth from the Father" (John 16:26-27). Jesus speaks of a day, probably after His ascension, when it will no longer be necessary for Him to request the Father on behalf of His disciples. The disciples will request the Father directly, and He will respond because of His love for those who have loved His Son and believed in His divine mission from the Father. What a privilege it is to make requests of our heavenly Father, knowing that He loves us and wants to meet our needs.

One day a small boy was having the time of his life digging a hole in his backyard. His digging was interrupted, however, when he came across a large stone. He loosened it from the surrounding dirt but couldn't lift it out of the hole. His father, watching the boy's efforts, finally said, "Are you using *all* your strength?" "Yes, I am!" the boy insisted! "No, you're not," said the father. "You haven't asked *me* to help you." We Christians are sometimes like this little boy. We have a source of strength in our heavenly Father that we often overlook. What an encouragement to know that we have direct access to the Father because of Jesus and our love for Him. Let's not overlook our *greatest* source of strength.

In verse 28, Jesus declares His heavenly origin and heavenly destination. "I came forth from the Father, and have come into the world; I am leaving the world again, and going to the Father," The last clause in verse 28 is better translated, "Again, I am leaving the world and going to the Father." This verse summarizes the life of Jesus—His mission, nativity, passion, and ascension. Hearing these words, the disciples immediately recognize that Jesus is now speaking plainly (16:29). They go on to confidently assert their belief that Jesus is from God. "Now we know that You know all things, and have no need for anyone to question You; by this we believe that You came from God" (16:30). The phrase, "and have no need for anyone to question You," refers to Christ's omniscience regarding the concerns of their hearts. He knew their questions even before they were spoken (16:19; cf. 2:24-25). Christ's full knowledge was, to the disciples, convincing evidence of His divine origin.

A Christian's Ultimate Victory (16:31-33)

The last section closes with the disciples' confession of faith, "By this we believe that You came from God" (16:30). The disciples' faith was undoubtedly genuine as far as it went, but Jesus knew that the limitations of their faith would soon be apparent. He answered them with the words, "Do you now believe?" (16:31) Grammatically the phrase can be understood either as a question ("Do you now believe?") or a statement of fact ("Now you believe." The word "now" (*arti*) regards the present situation in relation to the past or future. It could be translated, "At this moment," or "at the present time." Jesus is probably saying, "At this time you are trusting Me—but an hour of crisis is coming when your faith will be tested." Jesus was

180

not questioning the reality of the disciples' faith, just its power and steadfastness.

Jesus goes on to speak of the disciples' future failure. "Behold, an hour is coming, and has already come, for you to be scattered, each to his own home, and to leave Me alone; and yet I am not alone, because the Father is with Me" (16:32). Jesus recognizes that the long awaited "hour" (2:4; 7:6,30; 12:23; 13:1; 17:1) has virtually begun. The "hour" refers to that time when God would glorify the Son through His sacrificial death for our sins (cf. 12:23-24; 17:1). For Jesus, it would be an hour of crisis—a time when He would be spiritually separated from the Father. For the disciples, it would be a time of regrettable failure. Though they had professed faith in Christ and had committed themselves to Him (cf. Mark 14:31), they would all be scattered as sheep without a shepherd. Yet, in view of Christ's relationship with the Father, even when abandoned by the disciples, He would not be alone. The Father would be with Him. But there would come a moment on the cross when Jesus would cry out, "My God, My God, why have You forsaken Me?" (Matt. 27:46). As Jesus became sin for us, He was forsaken by God the Father as sin—past, present, and future—was laid on Him and judged.

How encouraging it is to know that the sacrifice for sin has been paid and that the Father will never "turn His back" on us. He Himself said, "I will never desert you, nor will I ever forsake you" (Heb. 13:5).

Jesus concludes His final word of encouragement to His disciples in John 16:33, revealing the purpose of His instruction and the certainty of His victory. Jesus' purpose is to deliver peace. His confidence is in His ultimate victory. Observe that verse 33 pictures the believing disciples as living within two spheres—eternal life in Jesus and temporal life in the world. Temporal life in the world will be characterized by "tribulation." Jesus is not speaking here of the seven-year Tribulation which will follow the Rapture of the church and precede the Second Coming. The word is used here in a general sense to speak of the "pressing affliction" or "trouble" which the disciples will endure as they identify with Jesus in an unbelieving world (cf. John 15:18-25). You and I experience this kind of "trouble" when we take a stand on sensitive moral issues or speak a word for Jesus in a hostile environment. How do we handle this "trouble" or "pressing affliction"? Jesus gives us the answer. In the *world* we have pressure, but in *Jesus*, disciples can experience peace. Though there is plenty of trouble in the world, there is an abundance of peace in Jesus. He Himself said, "Peace I leave with you; My peace I give to you" (14:27).

Finally, in the face of the cross, Jesus claims victory over a troubled, unbelieving world. He announces triumphantly, "I have overcome the world!" To unbelievers, the cross appears as an emblem of defeat; but Jesus sees it as a standard of victory! The most exciting truth to me is that we believers get to share in that victory! Christ has accomplished a victory in which all believers share by virtue of their identification with Him (Col. 2:12). Thus Paul is able to declare, "But in all these things we overwhelmingly conquer through Him who loved us" (Rom. 8:37). Elsewhere he rejoices, "But thanks be to God, who gives us the victory through our Lord Jesus Christ" (1 Cor. 15:57). John puts it all together for us when he writes, "For whatever is born of God overcomes the world; and this is the victory that has overcome the world—our faith. And who is the one who overcomes the world, but he who believes that Jesus is the Son of God" (1 John 5:4-5).

John the Baptizer was a man of confidence, conviction, and daring. He wasn't afraid to call sin "sin," even when it appeared in high places. Yet he had a considerable amount of what Jesus calls "pressing affliction" or "trouble" during his sojourn on earth. He was accused of being demon-possessed (Matt. 11:18), suffered arrest and imprisonment (Matt. 14:3), and was eventually slain at the whim of Herod's wife (Matt. 14:8-10). In spite of all this, John the Baptizer triumphed in life. Jesus Himself called John the greatest man who ever lived (Matt. 11:11). How was this possible? I believe that John knew that Jesus' triumph would be his victory.

Remember when his disciples were leaving John to follow Jesus? (cf. John 3:26) What an opportunity for the flesh to gain control and cause John to try to keep his followers for himself. But instead, John responded, "He must increase, but I must decrease" (3:30). John knew that it was his place to exalt the Master, for he would share in the Messiah's success. As a Christ-exalting disciple, you too share in Jesus' victory. In this world you will experience pressing affliction. But for all the disciples of Jesus, there is victory. These words will get you through more than a doctoral exam These are words of encouragement that will get you through life!

Study and Review Questions

1. What did Jesus mean by the words in John 16:16, "A little while, and you will no longer behold Me; and again a little while, and you will see Me"?
2. Must Jesus' disciples always be happy? (cf. 16:20,22) How do you distinguish between happiness and joy?
3. What are some of the ways believers can experience the joy which Jesus promised His disciples?
4. Why would it be unnecessary for Jesus to use figurative language in teaching the disciples after His resurrection? (16:25).
5. Why might verse 28 be designated a "biography of Jesus in a nutshell"?
6. Was the belief which the disciples affirmed in verse 30 sincere? How did Jesus view it?
7. What are the two spheres in which believers operate? (16:33) What is the characteristic of each.
8. Can a disciple of Jesus be assured of ultimate victory in life? What is the scriptural basis for a believer's victory?

Chapter 12

Prayer for 1st Century Disciples

John 17:1-19

John Sutter's expanding agricultural empire in California's Sacramento Valley needed lumber, and there was none in his vast domain. To solve this problem, Sutter appointed one of his workmen, James Wilson Marshall, to build a sawmill in the Coloma Valley, along the south fork of the American River in the foothills of the Sierra mountains. On the morning of January 24, 1848, while inspecting the progress on the millrace, Marshall spotted some shining specks in the water. He scooped them up, and after testing them with his fingernail and pounding them with a rock, hurried back to the mill and announced to his workmen, "Boys, I believe I have found a gold mine!" The great California Gold Rush followed in the wake of this announcement.

As we come to the study of John 17, with Marshall we must say, "I believe we have found a gold mine!" But unlike the mines in the Coloma Valley which have long been depleted, this one still yields treasure to those who are willing to probe its depths.

John 17 is the longest of our Lord's recorded prayers, and was probably spoken in the presence of the disciples somewhere on the way to the Garden of Gethsemane. The prayer divides naturally into three main sections—

Jesus' prayer for Himself (17:1-5), His prayer for His 1st century disciples (17:6-19), and His prayer for future believers (17:20-26). In this chapter, we will be focusing on Jesus' prayer for Himself and His 1st century disciples. Now, let's mine some of that gold!

Jesus' Prayer for Himself (17:1-5)

Jesus' prayer in the presence of His disciples is the culmination of all the words He spoke to them in His final discourse before the cross. John observed Jesus "lifting up His eyes to heaven" as He began the prayer. Lifting one's eyes—and sometimes one's hands—was a common posture for prayer in the biblical period (cf. Ps. 63:4; 123:1; Mark 7:34; John 11:41; 1 Tim. 2:8). These gestures signified the readiness of the petitioner to receive from God the answers to what they had requested in prayer.

Jesus prayed, "Father, the hour has come; glorify Your Son, that the Son may glorify You" (17:1). In keeping with the instructions Jesus gave His own disciples, He appealed to God as His "Father." This is the language of children would use to address their dads. The term "Father" suggests a close familiarity between Jesus and His heavenly "Father" and alludes to the fact that Jesus was totally submissive to His Father's will as an obedience son would submit to a parent. The word "Father" is also an expression of Christ's confidence that God would answer His prayer just as any earthly father would want to meet the need of his child. The importance of our being personally related to God as our heavenly Father is illustrated in the following story. Two young boys were playing in the street one hot afternoon when they saw the Popsicle man approaching. One boy pointed to his father who was working in the yard and told his friend, "Ask my dad if we can have money to buy Popsicles. The other boy responded, "I can't ask him. He's not my father!" If God is your spiritual Father, He will answer your prayer and meet your need just as He would for Jesus.

Jesus addressed the Father in light of the immediate prospect of His death on the cross. His time ("the hour") had come. Now, facing death on a Roman cross, Jesus petitioned the Father for a full restoration of His own pre-incarnate glory—that glory which He veiled when He took on human flesh and became a man. The word "glory" refers to the estimation in which one is held. It has to do with one's "reputation" and in this context would refer to Jesus' divine attributes. I believe that Jesus was praying for the Father to demonstrate His inherent divine nature through His victory over death. Note carefully that this request was not self-seeking. Jesus adds to His request, "that the Son may glorify You." Jesus glorification would not be an end in itself, but was a means to the greater glory of the Father. The motivation behind Christ's prayer was to enhance the Father's reputation.

In John 17:2, Jesus reveals the degree of the glorification He desires, "Even as You gave Him authority over all mankind, that to all whom You have given Him, He may give eternal life." Jesus desired to be glorified to the same degree that He had been delegated authority over all mankind—especially the authority to confer eternal life (cf. John 3:35-36; 5:24; 10:28).

Verse 3 contains the Bible's best definition of this "eternal life" which the Son has authority to confer. "And this is eternal life, that they may know You, the only true God, and Jesus Christ whom You have sent"(17:3). Eternal life is first of all a *quantity* of life, in that it precludes perishing (10:28). The expression "eternal life" is used frequently with reference to a believer's future destiny (3:36; 5:29; 12:25). But eternal life also has a present, *qualitative* aspect (10:10). Jesus has "life" in Himself and is a source of life to others (5:21,24,28). Jesus grants eternal life as a *present* possession to those who believe in Him. In John 17:3, this "eternal life" is equated with an intimate and personal knowledge of God the Father and Jesus the Son. Since the word "know" is present tense in the original Greek language, Jesus must be referring to an ever increasing knowledge rather than a stagnant body of doctrine. To know the Father through the Son is to fully participate in a never ending life with God!

Jesus declares in verse 4 that the Father has been glorified as a result of His earthly ministry. "I glorified You on the earth, having accomplished the work which You have given Me to do." Through the work Jesus accomplished on this earth, the glorifious reputation of God the Father was magnified. Speaking to His disciples at the well near the village of Sychar, Jesus said, "My food is to do the will of Him who sent Me, and to accomplish His work" (4:34). Now with the cross before Him, Jesus sensed the fulfillment of the task that had been assigned to Him. Soon He would announce from the cross, "It is finished" (19:30). Disciples can deduce a helpful principle from John 17:4. Jesus demonstrates through His life that

God is glorified by the accomplishments of His obedient servants. It is exciting to know that followers of Jesus can bring glory to God as we fulfill His calling and commands in our own lives.

In verse 5, Jesus clarifies and elaborates the request of verse 1. "And now, glorify Me together with Yourself, Father, with the glory which I ever had with You before the world was." Jesus prayed for a full restoration of His own pre-incarnate glory and renewed fellowship with the Father, both of which He had enjoyed within the Trinity throughout eternity past. In His transfiguration, Jesus gave Peter, James, and John a revelation of the future glory which He would enjoy in the kingdom (Matt. 17:1-2). Now as He concludes His life's work, Jesus prays that His full glory will be restored; that His divine attributes will be fully displayed as a means of enhancing the Father's reputation. The answer to this prayer was realized in Jesus' death, resurrection, and ascension (cf. John 21:19; Rom. 6:4; 1 Tim. 3:16).

Jesus' Prayer for 1st Century Disciples (17:6-19)

Having prayed for Himself, Jesus turns His thoughts toward the men God gave Him. In John 17:6-19, Jesus prays for His eleven faithful disciples. Before beginning His prayer, Jesus reflects on the spiritual status of these to whom the Father's reputation ("name") had been manifested through His life's work (17:6a). In a way, Jesus was taking a spiritual inventory of the lives of the eleven. They had *received* Christ's Word, *obeyed* His teaching, and *believed* in His divine origin from the Father (17:6b-8). What more could Jesus ask for? He was about to pray for those who were entrusted to carry the gospel message throughout the ancient world. They faced a monumental task, innumerable perils, and satanic opposition. What should He ask for? We discover here that Jesus asks the Father for just three things for His disciples. He asks that they would be (1) kept in His name, (2) protected from the evil one, and (3) sanctified in the truth (17:9-19).

Keep them in Your Name (17:9-13).

In verses 9 and 10, Jesus gives the reason for His first request. "I ask on their behalf; I do not ask on behalf of the world, but of those whom You have given Me; for they are Yours; and all things that are Mine are Yours, and Yours are Mine, and I have been glorified in them" (17:9-10). Jesus prays not for the unbelieving world, but for His little band of disciples. It is not that Jesus had little concern for the world, but rather He sense a special responsibility toward the apostles who would have such significant leadership roles in the early church. They needed prayer, and Jesus responded by interceding for their spiritual needs.

Christ's specific request is recorded in verse 11, "And I am no more in the world; and yet they themselves are in the world, and I come to You. Holy Father, keep them in Your name, the name which You have given Me, that they may be one, even as We are." This prayer was motivated by the fact that Jesus' departure was imminent. Jesus explains, "While I was with them, I was keeping them in Your name which You have given Me; and I guarded them, and not one of them perished but the son of perdition, that the Scripture might be fulfilled" (17:12). Jesus prayed for His own because He would no longer be on the earth to personally keep and guard the disciples.

190

His work on behalf of the Twelve had been successful and not one had been lost—except for Judas. And that one special case was according to biblical prophecy (cf. Ps. 41:9). The terms "perished" and "son of perdition (or *destruction*)" are antithetical to the concept of salvation and point to the fact that Judas was an unregenerate man (cf. John 10:28; 3:15-16; 2 Thess. 2:3; Rev. 17:8,11).

What did Jesus mean, "keep them in Your name"? In ancient times a "name" represented one's character or reputation. This has some carry-over into modern culture. My mother used to admonish me as a young teenager to do nothing that would bring dishonor to the Laney name. She was concerned that my activities not detract from the family reputation. God had entrusted His reputation to Jesus who revealed it to the disciples. Now Jesus prays that the disciples may be kept true to that revelation. The purpose of this prayer is that the disciples might share a unity of spirit modeled after the unity shared by the Father and the Son within the Trinity. This concept of unity will be further developed in John 17:20-26.

In verse 13, Jesus again reflects on His impending departure. "But now I come to You, and these things I speak in the world, that they may have My joy made full in themselves." Apparently Jesus prayed aloud so that the disciples would be comforted by the fact that He Himself had consigned them to His Father's keeping. Jesus wanted His disciples to continue experiencing a full measure of His joy.

Keep them from the Evil One (17:14-16).

Jesus' second request was that the disciples be kept "from the evil one." The motivation for this request is reflected in verse 14, "I have given them Your Word; and the world has hated them, because they are not of the world, even as I am not of the world." This thought is repeated in verse 16 for emphasis. In light of the hostility of the world toward believers who are separated from the world and identified with Christ (cf. John 15:18-25), Jesus prays that His own might be protected. The nature of this protection is made clear in the next verse: "I do not ask You to take them out of the world, but to keep them from the evil one" (17:15). Jesus did not pray that the disciples be removed from the world, for that is where they were needed. It is significant that Moses, Elijah, and Jonah all prayed to be taken out of the world, but in no case was the request granted (Nu. 11:15; 1 Kings 19:4; Jonah 4:3,8).

Jesus did not pray that the disciples be exempted from combat by being removed from the arena, but rather that they be kept from the permanent, overriding influence of the enemy. Some expositors believe that Jesus was simply praying for the disciples to be kept from evil. While this would be important, the definite article in the Greek text would indicate that Jesus was referring to *the* evil one—Satan himself (Matt. 5:37; 1 John 5:19). Jesus is quite aware of the activity of Satan and his dominion over the world. The Apostle John tells us that "the whole world lies in the power of the evil one" (1 John 5:19). Peter tells us that Satan "prowls about like a roaring lion, seeking someone to devour" (1 Peter 5:8). Paul exhorts us to "put on the full armor of God that you may be able to stand firm against the schemes of the devil" (Eph. 6:11). In His prayer for His disciples, Jesus recognizes the power of the devil and prays for His own to be kept out of his power and influence as they carry out their work in Satan's domain. While Satan is a powerful adversary, it is encouraging for believers to know that he is also a coward, for James said, "Resist the devil, and he will flee from you" (4:7).

Sanctify them in the truth (17:17-19).

Jesus' third request on behalf of His disciples was for their sanctification. "Sanctify them in the truth; Your Word is truth" (17:17). What does it mean to be sanctified? The Greek word translated "sanctify" literally means to be "set apart" for a special purpose. Certain vessels from the potter's shop were set aside for use by the priests officiating in the temple and became "holy vessels" (cf. Rom. 9:21). When my wife makes cookies for a church social, she separates out the nicest looking cookies—those that are not too light or dark—and takes them to church. The rest are left in the cookie jar at home for me to enjoy! Here we have "holy cookies"—those set apart from a common use to a special purpose. Sanctification, then, has the idea of "dedication" or "consecration" and in a spiritual context implies a separation from evil.

According to Scripture, there are three aspects to a believer's sanctification—past, present, and future. We are *positionally* sanctified when we trust Jesus as our Savior. Paul was able to refer to those problem prone Corinthians as "those who have been sanctified in Christ Jesus" (1 Cor. 1:2). Because of their position in Christ, they could be called "saints." Disciples don't always behave saintly, but by being declared righteous through

193

faith in Christ, they are indeed "saints." Then, believers are *experientially* sanctified as they "work out" their salvation with fear and trembling (Phil. 2:12). This refers to our being "set apart" from the power and influence of sin. Paul said, "For this is the will of God, your sanctification; that is, that you abstain from sexual immorality" (1 Thess. 4:3). Disciples will be *ultimately* sanctified when they see Jesus in their glorified bodies. Concerning this final aspect of a believer's glorification, John writes, "We shall be like Him, because we shall see Him just as He is" (1 John 3:2). The only aspect of sanctification that believers can do anything about is the *present* aspect or our sanctification, and that is precisely what Jesus prays about in verse 17.

Notice that the disciples' sanctification is to be done "in the truth"—the truth contained in the written Word of God. The term "in" suggests that the present aspect of a believer's sanctification is accomplished by the Word of God which is the embodiment of revealed truth. The Word of God is not only true, it is the very essence of truth (cf. 2 Tim. 3:15-16; 2 Peter 1:20-21). How is this present aspect of a believer's sanctification to be accomplished? I believe that the present aspect of sanctification will be accomplished in the lives of Jesus' followers when they yield to *God's Word* and *God's will* (Rom. 12:2; 6:12) by the power of the *Holy Spirit* (Rom. 8:3-4). By yielding to God's will and Word by the energizing power of the Holy Spirit, a believer's practice is brought into conformity with his or her position in Christ. One day when we meet Jesus in our glorified bodies, our sanctification will be complete.

Verse 18, which might appear parenthetical at first glance, develops the thought of verse 15—that the disciples will remain in the world. "As You sent Me into the world, I also have sent them into the world" (17:18). The mission of Christ forms a pattern for the mission of the apostles. As Jesus was sent with a task to discharge, so His apostles were sent into the world with a mission to accomplish. Yet while Christ was *in* the world, verse 19 reveals that He was not *of* the world. "And for their sakes I sanctify Myself, that they themselves also may be sanctified in truth" (17:19). How can the sinless Christ be "sanctified"? The key is the meaning of the word. While living in this world, Jesus "set Himself apart" from it to do the Father's will (Phil. 2:8) and thus provided, through His work on the cross, a basis for the disciples' sanctification. Through His sacrificial death, the way was prepared for the disciples to be "set apart" to God.

William Randolph Hearst (1863-1951), the American editor and publisher, spent colossal sums of money buying and building castles and filling them with fine art treasures. As he accumulated art objects from around the world, Hearst stored his treasures in large warehouses. The story is told that Hearst once asked his agent to purchase some fine European art objects that he was interested in. After an extensive search, the agent found the art treasures—in Hearst's own warehouse! Jesus' prayer for His disciples is a warehouse full of spiritual treasures. In your search for spiritual nuggets, don't overlook the storehouse of truth in Jesus' prayer for Himself and His disciples.

Study and Review Questions

1. What is the essence of Jesus' prayer for Himself in John 17:1-5? What does the word "glorify" suggest?
2. Define eternal life on the basis of what Jesus says in John 17:3. What aspect of "eternal life" is being considered here?
3. Jesus took a spiritual inventory of the disciples in John 17:6-8. How would you evaluate their faith at this point in their spiritual journey?
4. What did Jesus mean in His prayer, "Holy Father, keep them in Your name"? (17:11).
5. Was Jesus unable to keep Judas in the Father's name? Why did he perish? (17:12) Would you say that Judas lost his salvation, or is there an alternative explanation?
6. Did God answer Jesus' prayer of John 17:15? How does the Father "keep us from the evil one"? (17:15).
7. What does it mean to be "sanctified"? (17:17). How was Jesus "sanctified"? (17:19).
8. How can the present aspect of sanctification take place in your life?

Chapter 13

Prayer for 21ˢᵗ Century Disciples

John 17:20-26

Have you considered what a complicated piece of machinery your automobile is? Literally hundreds of moving parts and computer generated signals must work together with precision in order for the engine to function properly. A malfunction of just one part will result in something most all of us have experienced--car trouble!

Several years ago I set about rebuilding the motor for my 1942 WWII jeep. I dismantled the engine completely, replacing or refurbishing worn parts. It was a messy job working with lots of worn and oily seals, rings and springs. The most challenging part of the project was putting the motor back together again! I installed the crankshaft, piston rings, distributor, spark plugs, wires, carburetor and manifold. The big question lingering in my mind was, "Would it start?" Each part of that motor had to work smoothly with the other parts for it to start and run. If the motor didn't start, my time and expense would have been a wasted effort.

It was a suspenseful day when I tested the engine. I hooked up the battery and cranked the motor. It turned over, coughed, turned over some more, popped and *started running* on its own. After the blue smoke cleared from my garage, I stood there in amazement to see the motor running smoothly! Even with my limited experience of working on the motor, I have an increased appreciation for its mechanical functioning. I am sometimes amazed that the motor even runs at all, for in order to do so all the parts must be united and functioning together.

The body of Christ—the local church—is similar in a way to my jeep motor. The many different members with their unique gifts and abilities, must be united as one and functioning together for the church to be what Jesus intended it to be. This priority of *unity* in the body of Christ is the subject of Jesus' concern in John 17:20-26. In this chapter, we will consider the priority of spiritual unity reflected in Jesus' prayer for His 21st century disciples.

The Priority of Unity (17:20-23)

It was Jesus, not Abraham Lincoln in his Gettysburg Address, who first said, "A house divided against itself will not stand." Jesus made the statement to refute the Pharisaic view that He was casting out demons by the power of Satan (Matt. 12:24) rather than by the power of the Holy Spirit. He argued quite logically that Satan does not work against himself. Satan would not empower Jesus to cast out his demonic emissaries, for no kingdom, city, or house divided against itself can survive (12:25-26). Applying the truth of Matthew 12:24 to the church, we could say that division and disunity in the body of Christ diminishes its effectiveness and leads to its ruin. Fully appreciating the importance of unity in the church, Jesus prayed that those who believed in Him through the preaching of the apostles would share in spiritual unity. In other words, Jesus prayed for 21st century disciples. He prayed for us! "I do not ask in behalf of these alone, but for those also who believe in Me through their word; that they may be one; even as You, Father, are in Me, and I in You, that they also may be in Us; that the world may believe that You sent Me" (John 17:20-21).

Notice in verse 21 that the unity for which Christ prayed is a unity patterned after the unity shared by the Father and Son. In the Trinity there are multiple persons—the Father, the Son, and the Holy Spirit—but one divine essence, *one* God. (Deut. 6:4; Matt. 28:19; John 10:30). So too in the body of Christ, there are many members, but they share in a spiritual unity—a unity of the Spirit (1 Cor. 12:13).

In 1776, the Latin phrase *e pluribus unum* was suggested by Benjamin Franklin and Thomas Jefferson as aptly describing the creation of one nation out of thirteen colonies. Since 1873, federal law has required that the phrase appear on every coin minted by the U.S. Treasury. We often see it with the emblem of the eagle, our national bird. The phrase *e pluribus unum* is a perfect description of the unity shared by the members of the body of Christ. While there are many members in the community of Jesus' disciples, they are joined into a spiritual entity—the church. They are not many, but are *one*.

The purpose of the unity within the church—the body of Christ—is at least twofold. First, it is designed to promote fellowship with God. Jesus prayed that the believers would be unified so "that they also may be in Us" (17:21). The unity of believers allows them to share in a unity with the Father and Son. But the opposite is also true. Disunity among believers will hinder their individual fellowship with God. The second purpose of the believers' unity is evangelistic. Jesus prayed for the church to be unified "that the world may believe that You sent Me" (17:21). While the believers' unity has the potential to convince unbelievers of Jesus' divine mission to redeem and reign, it seems clear from the text that disunity among believers will hinder the advance of the Gospel.

Cyprian (ca. 200-258), the bishop of Carthage, offered this reflection about the importance of church unity. He wrote, "The oneness of the church is like the oneness of the sun; many rays, one light; like a tree having many branches, but one trunk, with its roots firmly fixed in the soil; or as when many brooks flow from one source, let the wealth of waters divide as they will, in their fountainhead they are one and the same. Take the ray from the sun, the oneness of the light suffers it not to be separated; break the branch from the tree, it withers; cut off the brook from its source, it dries up. The church of the Lord has the same unity and interdependence over all the world." Since disunity and division lead to spiritual disaster, the only alternative for the church is to strive for the unity for which Jesus prayed.

In order to promote this unity within the body of Christ, the "glory" given to Jesus has been granted to His followers. Jesus prayed, "And the glory which You have given Me, I have given to them; that they may be one, just as We are one" (17:22). What "glory" could Jesus be referring to? Some have understood this to refer to the glory believers will share with Jesus in heaven (2 Tim.

2:10; 1 Peter 5:10). Others understand Jesus to be speaking of the glory of a transformed life (2 Cor. 3:18). Still others take the "glory" to refer to the path of humble service (cf. Mark 10:35-45). Which of these options would result in unity among members of the body of Christ? It seems that sacrifice and service to the members of the body would best accomplish the objective of creating unity. The path of greatness through humble service is the "glory" which both Jesus and His disciples may share in.

Jesus looks to a day when future believers will be perfected into a unity which will impress the world with His divine mission and God's supreme love. Jesus continued His prayer, "I in them, and You in Me, that they may be perfected in unity, that the world may know that You sent Me, and You loved them, even as You loved Me" (John 17:23). Jesus again highlights the fact that our unity as believers can serve as a sign to the world confirming the truth of Christ's mission and God's redeeming love.

The World Council of Churches, an international association of 250 major Protestant, Catholic, Anglican, and Eastern Orthodox churches, was founded in Amsterdam in 1948. The purpose of the World Council of Churches is to foster cooperation and greater unity in the ecumenical sense in all the Christian churches in the world, whether Protestant or Catholic, liberal or conservative. Its activities embrace worship, evangelism, education, social and interracial justice, and international understanding and peace. Now, was the establishment of the World Council of Churches the answer to Jesus' prayer for unity? Did Jesus pray for an *organizational* unity which would lead to conformity and compromise of doctrinal commitments?

I am not convinced that the World Council of Churches as an organization represents the unity for which Jesus prayed.

First, the unity for which Jesus prayed was not *organizational*, but *spiritual*. Jesus prayed that His followers would manifest a spiritual unity like that which exists within the Trinity. It was an internal reality, not an outward organization, that Jesus desired for His future followers.

Second, the unity for which Christ prayed was not *uniformity*, but appreciative of *diversity*. True biblical unity recognizes the differences among believers who are equipped with a variety of gifts. Diversity is essential to the healthy functioning of the body of Christ. As Paul said, "Now you are Christ's body, and individually members of it" (1 Cor. 12:27).

Third, the unity for which Christ prayed is not merely *theoretical*, but finds expression in *practical* application. In acts 11:27-29, we read how the members of the church at Antioch recognized their unity with the church at Jerusalem. During a time of famine, the believers at Antioch sent relief to their needy brethren of Judea. The unity for which Jesus prayed is practical and bridges ethnic, geographical, social and even denominational boundaries.

It was Christmas day when I awoke early to the sound of sirens outside our apartment in Dallas, Texas. Seeing red lights flashing through our living room windows, I dashed outside to see if perhaps our building was on fire! I saw smoke billowing from the belfry of Scofield Memorial Church next door. Nancy and I had been members at Scofield since our arrival in Dallas to attend seminary. That Christmas morning, we watched the main auditorium go up in flames. The beautiful stained glass windows of Scofield Church were illuminated for the last time behind a wall of flame. It was a difficult time for the church family. So many memories were associated with that worship center—weddings, funerals, and baptisms.

The church members gathered at Chafer Chapel on the campus of Dallas Seminary for the first meetings after the fire. It was a congregation in mourning for the loss they had experienced just the week before. During the service, Pastor Neil Ashcraft read a letter sent to us from another Dallas church. The church was not affiliated with Scofield in any way, but the membership expressed their sorrow over the destruction of our worship center and enclosed a check for $1,000 to fund the rebuilding project. What a blessing to our congregation! This thoughtful deed was the practical application of a unity which was not organizational nor theoretical, but very practical and real. This expression of unity transcended denominational lines and was a source of great encouragement for the believers at Scofield Memorial Church. I believe this is the kind of unity Jesus prayed for in John 17:20, "that they may all be one."

Along the coast of northern California are great forests of redwoods—the giant sequoias. Redwoods are famous for their age, beauty, and fine wood. But one unusual characteristic of the redwoods is their tendency toward *unity*. Two redwood trees may grow up together several feet apart, and then after 50 or 100 years the trunks of the trees begin to touch. Quite often the bark begins to overlap and fill out so that the two trees ultimately become one! There are cases where a dozen trees have sprung up from the outer roots of a tree that has fallen and have formed a perfect circle. After several centuries these trees have grown together to that outwardly they appear as a single giant tree! In keeping with Christ's prayer, the goal of the body of Christ should be to grow into such a unity that the world will recognize us as one. The display of such unity in our individualistic society will be a testimony to the world of the divine Person and work of Jesus.

The Prospect of Fellowship (John 17:24)

Jesus' final petition for future believers is that they may be with Him in heaven to enjoy the splendor and majesty of His glory. "Father, I desire that they also, whom You have given Me, be with Me where I am, in order that they may behold My glory, which You have given Me; for You loved Me before the foundation of the world" (17:24). The word "behold" suggests sharing in and enjoying Christ's glory as the risen, ascended Son of God. Jesus' prayer that future believers will be with Him, beholding His glory, will certainly be answered, for it is part of God's divine plan for us.

Writing concerning the return of Jesus, the believers' "blessed hope" (Titus 2:13), Paul states, "Then we who are alive and remain shall be caught up together with them in the clouds to meet the Lord in the air, and thus we shall always be with the Lord" (1 Thess. 4:17). Note carefully the words, "We shall *always* be with the Lord."

How well I remember my courtship days with the girl who became my wife. We would share a special time going out for a pizza, taking a ride in my old Jeep, or just visiting friends. But each of those dates had to come to an end. I would take Nancy back to her sorority house and drive home alone. When we became engaged and began to plan our marriage, I looked forward to the time when we could say "good night" without having to say "good-bye." I have enjoyed such intimate companionship with Nancy for many years now. But I am certain that this is just a foretaste of the kind of blessed fellowship that believers will enjoy with Jesus throughout *eternity!* How I look forward to seeing the Master face to face. Then faith will be sight; what is wrong will be right; and we will behold the glory of Jesus *forever!*

The Concluding Benediction (John 17:25-26)

Jesus concludes His longest recorded prayer with a benediction calling attention to His mission and its accomplishment. Here Jesus addresses God as the "righteous Father," an epithet that calls attention to God's impeccable character and exercise of perfect justice. Jesus first acknowledges the world's ignorance of the Father. He prays, "O righteous Father, although the world has not known You, yet I have known You (17:25a). The world could not know the Father because it had rejected the Father's revelation in the Son. Jesus made it clear throughout His ministry that the only way to learn of the Father is through knowing the Son (1:18; 15:6).

But in contrast with the unbelieving world, the disciples had recognized Christ and His divine mission. Jesus continues, "And these have known that You sent Me; and I have made Your name known to them, and will make it known" (17:25b-26a). The disciples had, in a limited sense, come to know the person ("name") of the Father. They had more to learn, but they would be taught those things by the Holy Spirit (16:12-15). The goal of this future revelation of the person of Christ is twofold. Jesus explains, "That the love wherewith You loved Me may be in them, and I in them" (17:26b). Jesus desired that His own love might rule in the hearts of His disciples (13:34-35) and that He Himself might indwell them.

The last words of Jesus prayer, "I in them," sum up a thought that runs throughout Jesus' final discipleship instructions. Jesus is going away, and yet He will remain with His disciples. Having known Christ "according to the flesh" (2 Cor. 5:16), they would now be blessed with His spiritual presence. As Jesus told His disciples before His ascension, "I am with you always, even to the end of the age" (Matt. 28:19).

As I reflect on John 17:20-26, our Lord's prayer for future believers, I am confronted with the realization that the primary focus of His prayer for us is on *unity*. Yet as I look around, I face situations in my church, at my seminary, and among other Christian groups where the unity for which Christ prayed is not being realized. Is this because of secular influence? Has the church adopted the individualistic "do-your-own-thing" philosophy so prevalent in our modern world? Have Christians failed to follow the path of humble service ("glory") which is designed to lead to unity? Or has the Christian church simply overlooked the priority which Jesus placed on unity and turned its attention to other areas? Perhaps no one reason accounts for the apparent lack of unity in the Christian church today. But one thing we can know for sure. Our lack of unity will certainly hinder the advance of the Gospel and the cause of Christ. And yet it could be otherwise. The manifestation of our unity in the body of Christ could cause the world to know the gospel ("good news") message that God the Father has sent Jesus, His Son to be the Savior of the world (17:23).

Arthur Fiedler (1894-1979) was an American conductor who led the Boston "Pops" orchestra from 1930 to his death in 1979. He had an uncanny ability to orchestrate violins, horns, harps, and drums into one harmonious sound through which his listeners could appreciate the classic compositions of Bach, Beethoven, and other more contemporary musicians, including the "Beatles." Before a concert began, all the musicians would be busy tuning their instruments, and the resulting noise was something no one would ever mistake for music. However, when the concert began at the direction of the conductor, Arthur Fiedler, the musicians began working as one. They would perform in unity and harmony, but leave room for individual expression. I believe this is a beautiful picture of the way the body of Christ ought to function. Under the direction of Jesus, the Conductor, all the members may function as one! The unity for which Jesus prayed was not organization, but spiritual; not theoretical, but practical; not uniformity, but embracing diversity. The unity grounded in Jesus leaves room for a medley of actions and functions, the only real conformity being to the mind of Christ and the direction of the Spirit.

Study and Review Questions

1. For whom is Jesus praying in John 17:20-26?
2. What kind of unity did Jesus have in mind when He prayed, "that they may all be one"? (17:21).
3. What are some things which do not make for unity among believers in the local church? How can these things be avoided?
4. Explain the unity which exists within the Trinity. How does this correspond to the unity that should exist in the church?
5. What influence does Jesus expect this unity to have on the unbelieving world (17:23)?
6. What did Jesus petition the Father for in verse 24? Can you think of any reason Jesus would ask the Father for something He knew would come about anyway?
7. What practical steps can you take to promote unity among Jesus' disciples in your church? In your Bible study? In your home?

Epilogue: Principles for Disciples

Less than 24 hours after Jesus delivered His final discipleship instructions in the Upper Room, He was tried by the Jewish authorities, condemned by the Roman governor, crucified on a wooden cross, and buried in a borrowed tomb. The disciples who had promised never to leave Him, forsook Him and fled, just as Jesus had predicted. Then, on the first day of the week, Jesus arose from the dead and appeared to His disciples. As they came to believe in His resurrection, the lives of Jesus' 1st century disciples were radically changed! These followers of Jesus had received their final discipleship instructions from the Master Discipler. Empowered by the Holy Spirit, they were now prepared to carry the good news of His life and teachings throughout the Roman world.

What discipleship lessons have we gathered from Jesus' final instructions to His disciples? Listed below are the principles Jesus emphasized in the discipleship instructions which He taught eleven of his committed followers on the night before His death.

1. The essence of a disciple's ministry is serving others (John 13:1-10).

2. The motive for a disciple's ministry is his or her love for Jesus (21:15-17).

3. Setting one's affections and attention on the material things of life, to the exclusion of spiritual

matters, will result in disciple's disappointment and demise (13:28-30).

4. Agape love or sacrificial commitment is to be the distinguishing mark of Jesus' disciples (13:34-35).

5. Jesus will return one day to take His disciples to their heavenly home (14:2-3).

6. Only through Jesus and His sacrifice on the cross can any disciple gain entrance into heaven (14:6).

7. Jesus, the Master Disciple Maker, shares in one divine essence with God the Father (14:9).

8. Praying to the Father on the basis of the merits and influence of the Son is the key to effective prayer for Jesus' disciples. (14:13-14).

9. The measure of a disciple's love for Jesus is their obedience to His Word (14:15).

10. Disciples of Jesus have an ever present Helper in the Person of the Holy Spirit (14:16-17).

11. Disciples who love and obey Jesus, share in a unique fellowship with the Father, Son, and Holy Spirit (14:17,23).

12. Disciples may experience peace with God and inward contentment as spiritual legacies granted by Jesus (14:27).

13. Fruitfulness in the life of a disciple results from abiding in Christ (15:2).

14. Disciples enjoy friendship with Jesus as they know Him intimately and obey Him willingly (15:14-15).

15. The world's attitude toward Jesus' disciples is characterized by hatred and hostility (15:18-21).

16. The Holy Spirit serves as a co-witness with disciples concerning the Person and work of Jesus (15:26-27).

17. The Holy Spirit witnesses to the person of Christ by convicting potential disciples of sin, righteousness, and judgment (16:8-11).

18. The Holy Spirit functions as a teacher and guide, illuminating spiritual truth for Jesus' disciples (16:13-15).

19. Jesus' disciples might not always be happy, but they need never be lacking in real joy (16:20-22).

20. Jesus has accomplished a victory in which all His disciples share a part (16:33).

21. God will be glorified through the accomplishments of His obedient disciples (17:4).

22. Jesus' disciples are progressively sanctified by the Holy Spirit and through the Word of God, which is the embodiment of revealed truth (17:17).

23. Unity of disciples in the body of Christ is a spiritual priority which testifies to the world of the person and work of Jesus (17:21-22).

24. Jesus is present with His disciples now and they will be with Him forever (17:23-24).

Wow, this is a lot of truth for Jesus' disciples to assimilate!

There are two ways we can respond to Jesus' teaching. We can either hear and obey, or hear and turn away. Having studied Jesus' final discipleship instructions in His Upper Room discourse, you can become a forgetful hearer or an effectual doer of the Word (James 1:22-25). Which will it be for you?

For further study of the Gospel of John, see my commentary, *John: Moody Gospel Commentary*, published by Moody Publishers.

Made in the USA
Middletown, DE
01 September 2021

47362120R00119